Planning and Building Church Facilities

Gwenn E. McCormick

BROADMAN PRESS
NASHVILLE, TENNESSEE

5200-83

ISBN: 0-8054-3011-3

Dewey Decimal Classification: 726
Subject Heading: CHURCH ARCHITECTURE // CHURCHES
Library of Congress Catalog Card Number: 92-20576
Printed in the United States of America

Library of Congress Cataloging-in-Publication Data

McCormick, Gwenn E.
Planning and building church facilities / Gwenn E. McCormick.
p. cm.
ISBN 0-8054-3011-3
1. Church facilities—Planning. 2. Church architecture—Designs and plans. I. Title.
BV604.M33 1992
254′.7—dc20 92-20576
CIP

PLANNING AND BUILDING CHURCH FACILITIES

This book is dedicated to the lay persons who give so unselfishly of their time and resources to the process of planning and building facilities that enable their churches to function effectively in mission, ministry, and outreach. May their tribe increase.

CONTENTS

1

Leading Your Church to Build

Successful church building programs don't just happen. They are the results of good leadership, sound planning, and hard work. Churches that have good experiences with building projects do so because they make significant investments in the venture—investments of time, energy, financial resources, and personal commitment. These investments are so extensive that a church must guard against the tendency for the building program to become the major item on its agenda.

One way to keep building in its proper perspective is to have some basic guidelines to follow in the process. Leaders who have a sound plan, a clear idea of what to expect, and a strong sense of the church's mission will be able to lead successful building programs. They will lead committees to develop plans based on adequate surveys and studies. They will help create an atmosphere of confidence and expectation within the membership. They will help generate energy and excitement as the challenging task is implemented with vision and hope.

Few leadership roles in the church have the potential of such far-reaching effectiveness and long-term benefits as planning and building new facilities. Buildings that are well-planned, functional, and effective tools can bless a church for many, many years. Conversely, buildings that are poorly designed, inadequately planned, and improperly constructed can restrict and burden a church for generations. Successful building programs can help strengthen and enrich the fellowship and commitment of the entire congregation. They can help focus the church's energies and resources for more effective outreach and ministry.

They can help lift the church to the higher ground of fulfilled aspirations and dreams. What a challenge!

This book is written to give guidelines, ideas, suggestions, and directions for providing leadership in the building-planning process. The following chapters give details for developing the organization, doing adequate studies, working with design and construction professionals, and moving through the planning and construction process. The remainder of this chapter suggests some key issues involved in leading your church to build.

Begin Planning Early

Some months ago a letter came to a denominational church architecture department with a simple request. "We have scheduled ground breaking for a new building a week from next Sunday. Please send us some plans for the building." Obviously, the leaders in that church had little awareness of what is involved in planning well-designed church buildings. Ideally, a church building program should grow out of the church's long-range plans. In actuality, the impetus for the program often comes from a sudden awareness that the church is out of space.

Effective leaders will not allow a building project to slip up on the church. They will be visionary and farsighted, seeing the need and beginning the preparation for building well in advance. Time is needed to do comprehensive program planning. This kind of planning clarifies how the church sees itself, what it understands its mission to be, where it wants to go, and how it expects to get there. No committee can do comprehensive program planning in one short meeting. Studies, surveys, and projections must be made, and these take time. Program planning must be completed before facility planning begins. The church that tries to design a new building before it clearly understands its program plans may make serious and costly mistakes in the process.

Once the church has formulated program plans, it needs help to translate these into floor plans for buildings. This, too, takes time—time for professionals to do space planning; time for church leaders to review and evaluate proposals; and time to study proposed designs for function and flexibility. Worship and educational leaders will need to "walk through" the proposed designs to see how they will function. The issue of function should not be left exclusively to architects and engineers; they may not understand how the church functions in all of its activities and ministries.

Early planning is also essential to allow time for capital fund-raising. A church can raise more money for a building in the months leading up to and during construction than at any other time. Since this is the optimum time for fund-raising, adequate allowance should be made in the schedule for this to be done well. Ideally, a capital-fund program should be conducted at least two years before the new building will be completed. Churches could save millions of dollars in interest and avoid staggering long-term indebtedness if they followed this advice. Unfortunately, church leaders often wait too late, and then find themselves saying, "We just don't have time for a capital-fund program. We must build now." Such haste usually leads to inadequate planning, poorly-designed buildings, and excessive costs.

Another reason for early planning is to allow time for adequate communication, deliberation, and congregational decision making. Congregations need to be fully informed about issues so they can make intelligent decisions. People need to know why a building is needed. They need to know what kind of space it will provide, what programs it will support, what it will cost, and how the church will pay for it. Leaders who shortcut this process will likely contribute to confusion, misunderstanding, and a divided church. Take care not to rush the building program so fast that many church members feel confused and left out of the process. Give people time to work through the issues and be a part of the challenging task.

Get Off to a Good Start

A good start in the building-planning process involves making a strong case for the facility being planned. This process touches the whole issue of motivation. Why do the leaders want to construct the building? How will it impact the life and work of the church? What contributions will it make to the church's mission? Keeping the project tied closely to the growth and mission of the church will help establish a proper motive for building. However, the relationship between the building, growth, and mission must be authentic.

Leaders in a building program should be models of integrity in dealing with the congregation. They should be discreet in the way they build the case for needing a new building. For instance, leaders should be careful when they establish the motivation for building on the basis of saturation of existing space. The perception that present space is not yet filled may be widely held by the congregation. Leaders need to deal with this perception and help members understand that the key issue is providing space for growth rather than filling every space every Sunday.

If growing age-group areas are saturated and no reassignment of space can correct this, new space may be needed. However, the saturation rule for building space should be used intelligently. This rule simply states that when average attendance is 80 percent of capacity, the building has reached its saturation point. At that point, unless the church provides either multiple services or more space, it will not likely maintain its growth. The church that only occasionally has an attendance of 80 percent capacity is not saturated. The point of the rule is that average attendance at 80 percent capacity represents basic saturation. In order to achieve that average, attendance frequently will have to run considerably above 80 percent. The rule does not mean growth stops as soon as attendance first reaches 80 percent capacity.

Indeed, some churches reach 95 to 105 percent capacity and still continue to grow. They go to multiple services or find space for people and continue to do things that generate growth. Never tell your people the church cannot grow any more until you get a new building. If you tell them that, the prediction may become a self-fulfilling prophecy. A church that wants to grow and does those things which produce growth will find ways to grow even when their space is saturated. They will rent space, borrow space, bring in temporary space, and in other ways be creative in finding space for growth.

Another factor involved in getting off to a good start is developing building plans on the basis of adequate data: surveys, community studies, and needs assessments. Introduce the building project with documentation of people needs, ministry needs, and outreach challenges rather than with an emphasis on building. Building should be the church's response to these needs and challenges. It is a part of the church's strategy for reaching people and meeting needs. Keep these points in central focus, and attention will be directed to highly acceptable reasons for the building project.

Prioritize Your Building Needs

Many churches start out with larger building plans than they are able to complete in the next project. As the planning progresses and cost estimates are made, they soon discover they cannot build as much as they had originally intended. How does a church decide what to include in the building project? Some make the decision in response to the prevailing sentiment within the congregation. Some make it on the basis of the pastor's recommendation. The decision should be made on the basis of priority church planning.

Such planning begins with a church developing a growth-ministry strategy. Through a process of study, evaluation, and prayer, a church decides what its major growth-ministry emphasis will be. Then it develops what it considers the best strategy for supporting that emphasis. No church can do everything its members feel should be done. A church cannot effectively implement every possible growth strategy. A church must decide where to put its weight down and how it will invest its energies and resources. How will growth be achieved? How will it be sustained? Many churches find that the Sunday School is their most effective tool for outreach and growth. A few churches grow primarily because of the charisma and dynamic preaching of the pastor. The most successful churches are those whose growth strategies involve a strong and effective Sunday School and dynamic worship services.

Every church needs to adopt a growth strategy before deciding what to build next. Once the strategy has been formulated, the leaders can then prioritize the building plans that will help implement the strategy. Keeping the strategy as the central issue in the planning process will help leaders decide what kind of space they need most. The critical concern is not what kind of building leaders want but what kind of building will undergird the church's growth strategy most effectively.

Buildings, like tools, are instruments for getting a job done. The kind of tools one needs depends on the job to be done. Selecting the tools before one knows what the job is can result in a total failure. The tools may be the best money can buy, but if they do not fit the job, the work will not go well.

Too often, churches build in response to sentiment or popular expectation. As a result, the building that is constructed does not meet the strategy needs of the church. In order to be most effective, a church needs the kind of space that will help it implement its growth-ministry strategy. Leaders need to accept the responsibility of teaching the congregation that there is a connection between the right kind of space, growth, and effective ministry. Therefore, the church's intentions for growth and ministry become the key issues in deciding what kind of building is needed.

Use the Building Emphasis to Grow the People

Studies and evaluations utilized in successful building programs provide excellent opportunities to deepen congregational understanding of the mission and work of the church. Wise leaders recognize these opportunities and the teachable moments they create. For instance, a church is struggling with the decision of whether to build a worship center or educational space next. The average lay person, with little understanding of the principles of church growth, thinks that an impressive worship facility is the key to growth. Effective leaders help members test such assumptions and give them adequate information for making an informed decision. Studies generally show that growth for many churches is related more directly to the effectiveness of the educational program than to the worship service. Therefore, the church that wants to grow will see that growth provisions are made for Sunday School as well as for worship attendance.

A building program provides unique opportunities for growing and stretching people in stewardship. Some members who have never pledged to the church budget can be led to make a pledge to the new building. This is one reason capital-fund programs are so important to a building emphasis. These programs often secure pledges from 60 percent of the families in the church. The average budget campaign may only secure pledges from 35 percent of the families. A person who pledges to the building program and has a fulfilling sense of participation in it may never return to his former level of sporadic support of the church. Therefore, the building program should be a time for developing deeper stewardship participation. The church that misses this opportunity may have difficulty bringing some of its members to a significant level of financial participation. This fact alone is sufficient reason for conducting an effective capital-fund program.

Another opportunity in a building program is the growing of people toward maturity in personal relationships. Building programs introduce a number of potentially divisive issues: whether or not to buy additional property, what type facility should be constructed, how the project will be financed, and architectural style and design. Members will need to study, debate, deliberate, pray, decide, and then move ahead with the project. Capable leaders will keep the focus on issues, not individuals. Mature persons will recognize that not everyone will agree on every decision. The church should deliberate, make a decision in faith, accept it, and move forward without antagonism or recrimination.

Don't expect this to happen as a natural part of the building process. Wise leaders will help set the stage for this kind of response by keeping the emphasis on wholesome personal relationships. Members will need to be reminded that the goal of the process is not to erect a structure but to build up the church as the family of faith so it can fulfill its mission. If constructing a facility divides the church, the entire process can end in failure.

Never Let the Building Become the Main Thing

Building programs can be like dinosaurs—gobbling up everything in their path. They can consume time, resources, attention, and concern. Evangelism, outreach, ministry, and mission must be kept on the front burner. If they are sidetracked, the spirit and vitality of the church will suffer. As important as the new building is, it is not the most urgent concern for the church. Reaching people, developing disciples, ministering in the spirit of Christ—these are at the heart of the church's purpose.

Effective leaders will keep the focus on these central issues. They will recognize that buildings don't grow churches nor do they make churches successful. The vitality of the church is dependent upon relational, spiritual, and biblical commitments. Keep these strong and the church will be vibrant and alive. Neglect these, promote the building program as the primary issue, and the church will suffer.

Leading your church in a building program is a challenging task. If you accept the challenge and commit yourself to do it effectively, your contributions will enrich and bless the church for generations to come. God can use you in this process to make a significant impact for His kingdom. Do the job well and you will find this a rewarding and satisfying experience. Think of the joy and satisfaction you can receive for years to come as this carefully planned building is used for the glory of God and the growth and effectiveness of his church. This kind of challenge calls forth the best in planning, preparation, and participation. Let this worthy investment motivate you to give your best.

2

Developing the Organization

One of the most important steps in the building-planning process is selecting leadership for an organization to guide the church through the entire project. Most churches do not construct buildings often enough to know from experience just what this entails. Therefore, leaders should be open to learning from the experiences of other churches. Churches can gain significant insights through both positive and negative experiences of other churches in organizing and building church facilities. Too often, in the midst of the process, leaders find themselves bogged down or stymied because they unwittingly set up a flawed organization. Now they see this and would like to make an organizational adjustment in an effort to move beyond the impasse. However, any time a church has to adjust its building-planning organization in the midst of the process there is always the possibility of negative fallout. The wise course is to follow the best recommendations for establishing an effective organization to give leadership throughout the entire process.

General Principles to Follow

1) Plan for Broad Participation from the Congregation

Some people argue that a small committee of no more than five persons should be responsible for all the planning and recommendations. There are, of course, several benefits to a small committee. It is usually easier to control and may work faster than a large group. However, when most of the work is done by a small committee there can be real difficulty securing the kind of congregational involvement essential in church building planning. A good principle to remember is people involved in planning have a strong sense of ownership in a project. Church members need to be involved in the planning process to prepare them to significantly support the building venture. This sense of involvement can come from serving on the committee or a workgroup, or from listening sessions and town-hall-type meetings.

The size of the committee, in the final analysis, should be determined by the size of the church and the scope of the building project. Remember that decisions for a church building project should be broadly based. If the entire church is expected to support the project financially, the entire church should be represented in the planning process. All ages, all interests, and all viewpoints should be represented in planning. Generally, a more representative planning group secures greater church support.

2) Select Committee Leadership with Great Care

The most important qualification is unquestionable involvement and loyalty in the life and work of the church. Leaders should exhibit a pattern of faithful support of the total church program. They should share the church's vision. Sometimes fringe members are asked to serve on this committee in the hope this will lead to their more active involvement in the church. This can create real problems. These persons may not be spiritually mature enough to handle the complex issues this committee will face. They may not have broad enough experience in the total life of the church to make wise decisions about facility planning. This is not a committee to which new or inexperienced church members should be assigned.

Another mistake in selecting committee members is assuming technical and vocational skills qualify persons for work on the committee. Churches may assume persons with financial or building experience are thereby qualified for this committee. These persons may be valuable committee members if they possess the qualifications referred to in the preceding paragraph. However, if their only qualifications are in technical or vocational areas, they should not be placed on the committee. (They may be consulted or in other ways involved at strategic times in the process but should not be on the building-steering committee.)

For instance, a good banker who is only casually associated with the church cannot be expected to provide the kind of visionary financial leadership needed. Indeed, he may be a real liability in the planning process because of a lack of vision and commitment. A building contractor who attends church only occasionally can hardly be expected to understand the specific needs for an educational building or a worship center. He may know how to put the structure together but may be completely ignorant of the program space needs of the church. His lack of church program experience may make him a negative influence.

People who are deeply involved in the programs of the church are needed on this committee. The best rule to follow is to select leaders who have the spiritual maturity, church involvement, and Christian dedication that will benefit this responsible group.

3) Define Assignments and Responsibilities at the Outset

When the church elects a committee to give leadership to the building-planning process, it should give the committee a clear statement of responsibility. Just what is the committee elected to do? What authority does it have? The committee might be instructed to provide leadership in securing adequate data about the church, the community, and growth possibilities; to provide guidance in planning the appropriate response the church should make to this data with regard to programs, ministries, and facilities; and to give direction to the design and construction of facilities that will support the church's mission. They might be directed to report back to the church and secure approval before proceeding beyond certain points. A clearly stated assignment is essential to the committee as it works. If the scope of the assignment is defined in advance, both the committee and the church will know what is expected.

4) One Committee/Council Provides Continuity

In some churches a long-range planning committee initiates the building-planning process. Other churches start with a feasibility or study committee and later elect a building committee to complete the assignment. Still other churches elect several committees which function independently during the building-planning period. These types of organizations can lead to duplication, omission, and a lack of continuity in the building process. One committee may erroneously assume another committee has already dealt with an issue. A committee may not support the recommendations of the preceding committee. Multiple committees functioning separately may make decisions before all the data is in and block a decision within the assignment of another committee. For instance, a finance committee might vote to limit the building budget before the church growth and program subcommittees decide what building capacity to recommend.

Organizational Models

The most effective organization is one that establishes a building-steering committee or a council whose members then become heads of subcommittees assigned specific areas of work. In this book, this group is referred to as the building-steering committee. The following models, based on church size, will help churches organize their committees. The models begin with the large church, involving the most comprehensive organization, and then move on to the medium-size and the small church.

1) Large Church

The building steering committee is made up of the following:

- Chairperson
- Secretary
- Chairpersons of eight subcommittees:
  - Promotion
  - Church growth
  - Church program
  - Property
  - Finance
  - Furnishings
  - Building plans
  - Construction

The committee is responsible for providing leadership and guidance throughout the entire process of survey and data collection, planning and program development, and designing and constructing the new building. This steering committee receives reports and recommendations from all subcommittees, refines and balances them, and develops recommendations to the church concerning the total project.

Every building-related issue with which the church deals goes through this committee. Under no circumstances does a subcommittee or a workgroup go directly to the church with recommendations. The only way to control and monitor the building project effectively is to centralize the decision-making process. If all recommendations are routed through the steering committee, this group can maintain balance and control for the entire project. Without this control, a strong subcommittee might go to the church and gain approval for a provision that would be completely out of balance with other aspects of the project.

The building-steering committee will likely receive some visionary recommendations they cannot implement. Their responsibility is to review and evaluate all recommendations and compile a building package for the church to consider. The package should be challenging and visionary, yet practicable. It should provide answers to the what, why, when, and how questions of the building project.

Remember that members of the building-steering committee become the chairpersons for the subcommittees which work on the project. Subcommittees are needed for the following areas:

- Promotion/publicity—keeps the building program before the congregation and the community.
- Church growth—accumulates adequate data on growth possibilities and projections and recommends appropriate strategies.
- Church program—studies the programs and ministries of the church and recommends actions in response to the church growth subcommittee's findings and related program needs.
- Property—evaluates existing property and deals with issues related to acquiring additional property.

• Finance—develops arrangements for capital fund-raising, interim and long-term financing, and financial packaging for the entire project.

• Furnishings—inventories and evaluates existing furnishings; determines what new furnishings are needed, orders these, and sees to their placement prior to the occupancy date.

• Plans—works with the architect in the process of developing complete construction plans and specifications for the new facility.

• Construction—works with the architect and contractor during the time of construction and is involved in the final inspection and acceptance of the building.

Details about the assignments for each of these subcommittees are found in appendix A.

2) Medium-size Church

All eight areas of subcommittee work just listed are important to a thorough building-planning process. However, projects of a medium-size church don't generally require as large an organizational structure. In most situations, these churches may want to combine several subcommittees. The following combinations often work well:

Church growth and church program subcommittee
Property and furnishings subcommittee
Finance subcommittee
Plans and construction subcommittee

Combining these subcommittees must not reduce planning and evaluation. Each subcommittee should work with vision and diligence to cover the total scope of the project.

3) Smaller Church

The smaller church may simplify the organization even more by eliminating subcommittees altogether. A committee of the following five leaders might be chosen:

Sunday School director
Chairperson of deacons, elders, or church board

Chairperson of finance committee
Chairperson of women's organization
Member-at-large

If the organizational plan for the smaller church is adopted, the committee should study the eight subcommittee responsibilities and be certain to address those issues which apply to their project. One of the risks of simplifying the organization is that important areas of work might be overlooked. The fact that a building project is small does not diminish the importance of comprehensive planning and evaluation. In fact, the smaller church may have a more pressing motivation for such planning than the large church. The fact that the building being considered may be the only structure built for many years is sufficient motivation to do adequate planning. Experience indicates that the smaller church is likely to err by failing to comprehend the importance of total facility planning and design. For example, a smaller church wants a new fellowship hall, and proceeds with plans with no thought about other needs, such as Sunday School space. The leaders do not seem to realize a building program creates an opportunity to upgrade space provisions. This may be the last opportunity for many years a smaller church will have to do this.

Use Workgroups

In addition to the subcommittees, some projects will be of sufficient size to use workgroups for specific assignments. A church that is constructing a large educational building and a fellowship hall might divide the church program subcommittee into the following workgroups:

Preschool division workgroup
Children's division workgroup
Youth division workgroup
Adult division workgroup
Church media library workgroup
Fellowship hall workgroup
Kitchen workgroup
Weekday activities workgroup

Church offices workgroup
Church music workgroup

The smaller and medium-size church will combine many of these workgroups just as they combined the subcommittees of the building-steering committee. For example, they might have an educational space workgroup and a fellowship hall workgroup. However, combining workgroups should in no way diminish the importance of adequate planning and preparation in each assigned area. Leaders should be on guard against the tendency to oversimplify the planning process.

Better that a church appear overorganized in its building process than that the planning for any area suffer from lack of focus and attention. It is cheaper and more sensible to organize adequately than to rebuild or rework structures improperly designed because no one took the time to determine specific needs for a particular area of the facility.

Plan Adequate Training Sessions

The building-steering committee, the subcommittees, and the workgroups will need orientation and training periods. Training sessions should be timely planned. The steering committee will need an orientation session before they form subcommittees. The subcommittees will need training before they organize workgroups. Each person needs to understand the assignment given, the timetable in which each group will function, and the procedure for making reports and recommendations.

Giving people information at the beginning will help keep the entire process on track. It will also reduce misunderstanding regarding procedures. The training sessions should create a sense of teamwork and establish a level of trust and cooperation for the process. Each group will need to feel its recommendations are fairly and objectively heard by leaders who bring a comprehensive focus to the entire project.

Of course, some subcommittees and workgroups will not begin their work for several months. Therefore, the intensive training for these groups may be scheduled closer to the time they will actually be expected to function. However, there is wisdom in including these subcommittees in an overall orientation process so they will have a clear understanding of what to expect. They can be informed during the orientation how and when their assignment plugs into the planning.

Consult appendix A for the assignments and functions of the subcommittees and workgroups. This material can become the basis for the training sessions and orientation period. Each subcommittee and workgroup chairperson needs a copy.

3

Doing Adequate Studies for the Project

One of the most difficult tasks of the building-planning process is securing appropriate, adequate, and essential information. The difficulty stems not so much from the fact that the information is hard to secure as from the fact that leaders do not understand its importance. Why make such a big deal about planning a new building? Doesn't the leadership of the church know what is needed? Isn't it fairly simple to design church facilities? Why waste time doing surveys and background studies? These and related questions clearly indicate some people don't feel much study and evaluation are needed prior to involvement in building construction.

Those who question the importance of extensive studies before starting construction should read the biblical accounts of the planning for the tabernacle and the temple. (See Ex. 35—39; 1 Kings 5—6; and 2 Chron. 3—4.) These passages clearly emphasize the significant amount of planning and background preparation that preceded the actual construction. The assumption that church building doesn't need adequate planning finds no support in these Old Testament models.

Sometimes church folk are slow learners. Jesus said, "The children of this world are in their generation wiser than the children of light" (Luke 16:8, KJV). Business enterprises make exhaustive studies before expanding their retail outlets. They want to know about shopping habits, standards of living, family incomes, housing developments, economic conditions, traffic flow, and numerous other issues. They are interested in social, economic, and real-estate changes in process or anticipated. Business leaders have learned they cannot succeed in business in isolation. Factors affecting a business's location also affect the success or failure of the enterprise.

Why are church leaders so slow to recognize this is also true for the church? For example, a church is situated in an area that is rapidly becoming industrial. Yet the leaders recommended a large worship center be built to double the seating capacity. The building was constructed, but five years later the church had even fewer people in worship than before the new building was erected. Would adequate studies have revealed trends that might have changed the church's plans?

Another church considered constructing an activities building as a means of outreach. Extensive studies indicated several pertinent facts:

1. Families in the church were already so deeply involved in recreational activities in the community they did not have time to participate in recreational programs at church.
2. The city recreational program was so complete and extensive there was little prospect of attracting unchurched folk to a church recreational facility.
3. The cost of staffing and operating the proposed facility would place a serious strain on the church budget.
4. There was a significant increase in the number of senior adults in the community and no organized program designed specifically for them.

In view of these and related findings, church leaders decided to design and build a facility for senior adult day care and activities. Once constructed, the facility was immediately successful. The church employed a minister of senior adults and found an excellent avenue for outreach. Through this program many families are now being touched with the good news of God's love and concern. This illustrates the value of adequate study and analysis in the process of building and planning.

The studies and survey work needed are largely determined by the building project being considered. Simple projects need limited studies. Complex projects require comprehensive studies. Projects involving new ministries and new directions should receive exhaustive study and evaluation. The committee must determine that a definite need exists for the new ministry in the community. It must also evaluate the church's readiness for involvement in that kind of ministry.

Kinds of Information Needed

1) People Information

People and their needs are at the heart of the mission and work of the church. Buildings are planned and constructed to meet people needs. Therefore, the church should know some things about the people in their area:

- Is the population growing, stable, or decreasing, and at what rate?
- What is the trend in age-group population—preschool, children, youth, and adults?
- How many people in the area are unchurched?
- Is church growth keeping up with the population growth in the area?
- What do people perceive to be the greatest church ministry need in their area?
- What type of programs or ministries are most appealing to the people?

2) Church Information

The congregation involved in issues of church building planning needs to have some comprehensive information about itself. At this point many leaders make a serious mistake. They assume the congregation really understands who they are as a church—that they are really in touch with the dream and mission of their church. Test that assumption and in many instances it will be found false. The average congregation does not have a focused, clearly defined understanding of itself. It may not be keenly aware of its history and heritage. Therefore, leaders need to help the congregation clarify some internal issues. They should help the congregation deal with the following questions:

- Who are we as a church?
- What is our primary business?

- Why are we here?
- How are we going to achieve our mission?

3) Community Information

Since the average church has its primary base of operations in a particular community, the church should have some basic information about that community. The church needs to know about the economic, social, health, educational, moral, and religious conditions in the community. Knowledge about commercial, residential, and recreational developments planned for the community is important. The church must also be aware of community resources.

Once a church has a comprehensive knowledge of the community, it is in a better position to determine the response it wants to make to these conditions. For instance, when a church discovers residential growth in the community will be primarily in high-rise apartment complexes, this becomes an important factor for church planning. If a church finds the illiteracy rate is high in the community, this suggests a type of ministry the church may want to initiate. If there is a pressing need for senior adult day care, the church may want to launch that kind of program.

Studies Should Be Mission-Driven

These studies can give the church adequate information for planning, developing goals, and determining directions. They are mission-driven. As information is gathered, the leaders should rediscover the church's dream or envision a new dream for the church. Every building-planning committee needs time to dream. When a group has permission to dream it unleashes energy. Some dreams will have to wait for the right time. Others will mesh perfectly with the present situation. Information from the studies shows the committee opportunities waiting to be claimed—challenges they dare not ignore. The studies are not data-driven. Their purpose is to uncover information that will help focus and clarify mission. Sometimes information is gathered and then not used effectively because the committee does not understand the connection between the data and planning. The committee must focus on the relationship between adequate data and the church's mission.

Focus On a Growth-Mission Strategy

Early in the planning process the steering committee should look closely at the church's mission statement. If there is no clearly articulated mission statement, the committee should request church leaders develop one. A mission statement speaks to the who, why, what, and how questions referred to earlier. It really deals with the question, "What is our mission, and how will we fulfill it?" The mission statement expresses in simple and straightforward terms the essence of the church's purpose.

After the mission statement is adopted, church leaders should formulate a growth-ministry strategy—the assumption being that both growth and ministry are involved in the mission statement. The growth-ministry strategy is an essential step in building planning. The church should define its strategy so facilities can be designed to support that strategy. Assume that the mission statement makes growth a priority concern. Church leaders must then struggle with the question, "How will we achieve our growth goals?" Churches do not grow just because a committee expresses concern. They must apply well-defined principles of church growth and evaluate various growth strategies. However, the church that tries to implement all these strategies may end up with fragmentation and failure. Usually, churches grow because they do two or three key things well, not because they do everything perfectly.

One of the problems with much church planning is that the committee focuses on the church's weaknesses. The group may discuss what the church is not doing that it needs to do. As a result, a kind of cafeteria list is drawn up of all the church needs to consider doing. Then as many as ten or twelve goals may be adopted. As the church tries to reach these goals, it diffuses its energies, and there is little chance of success.

The wiser course of action is to concentrate on the church's strengths. Identify its positive and powerful assets and find ways to build on them. Then expand into areas touched by the strengths. This involves a kind of selective discipline that enables leaders to say, "We will major on our strengths and simply accept the fact that we cannot do everything." This is one way a church identifies its gifts and claims them for effective service.

Developing a growth-ministry strategy enables the church to focus on the means by which growth is achieved. Then the church makes decisions about facility development on the basis of that strategy. The strategy is not just a beautifully articulated statement; it becomes the marching orders for the church. It is the criteria the church applies to the priority of space provisions. For instance, if the strategy is to grow through a strong, effective Sunday School, growth space for Sunday School becomes the number one space priority, even though a new recreation building or fellowship hall might be appealing.

Some committees talk about church growth and agree that Sunday School space is needed. Then they turn around and make a decision about a new building based on sentiment rather than strategy. The steering committee should guard against this tendency by insisting that every decision about a new building be directly tied to the growth-ministry strategy of the church. Until committees learn to insist on this connection, they will continue to recommend facilities that do not provide growth space. In doing so, they actually sabotage the church's growth-ministry strategy.

Avoid Data Determinism

One of the perils of the kind of comprehensive studies suggested in this chapter is that committees will allow the data to have the last word. Some committees assume the more information they obtain the more they will know about what the church should do. Later they discover the mass of information they have gathered has left them confused and bewildered. Even worse, it may leave them victims of a deterministic attitude. For instance, they discover the community is losing population, and there is little possibility of reversing the trend. The committee then assumes all this determines the church must suffer the same fate. Another church finds its area growing at such a rate the committee assumes the church will grow no matter what they do. Neither of these assumptions is justified by the facts. In truth, many churches are growing at encouraging rates in communities losing population, while other churches have plateaued or declined in communities growing at a significant rate.

When the surveys have been completed and the information analyzed, the committee must do more than interpret the results. The committee must become a strategic planning group of visionary disciples. They will note the results of the studies. They will observe the direction of the trends. They may even go so far as to say, "All this indicates we can expect. . . ." But they will not stop there. They will ask the Lord what they can do to lead their church. They will make a response of faith, daring to believe that the God who led His people through the wilderness in the Old Testament story is still leading His people today. He can make a way for them. He has resources that community surveys do not uncover.

This does not mean the committee will dismiss the trends or discount the information. It simply means they will not allow these things to have the last word. They will use the lessons from the studies to plot strategies and responses that can reverse trends and change directions. They will let the studies instruct but not limit them.

They will be sensitized by the data but will not allow it to weaken their resolve to fulfill their mission.

4

Dealing with Property Issues

Selecting property for a church site can be a challenging and complex task. The entire process has become more complicated in recent years because of zoning and environmental impact issues. No longer can a church simply locate a site, purchase it, and proceed at will to build on it as they desire. A church in Arizona purchased a two-acre site in an affluent neighborhood, and then discovered zoning would not allow them to build there. They went through the time-consuming process of trying to get zoning changed without success. Finally they had to accept the fact that they would have to find another location. A church in Florida purchased twenty acres of property in preparation for relocation. When they tried to get permits for site preparation and building they discovered that fifteen acres were classified as wetlands. That ruling left them only five acres for buildings and paved parking. These and other horror stories about property selection prove that committees must learn to do a more thorough job of research and evaluation before they purchase a site. This chapter focuses on the major concerns which should be considered in the process.

Characteristics of a Good Church Site

1) Community Viability

A good location for a church is one that has a large concentration of people or one that is easily accessible to a large number of people. Therefore, a church is well-advised to locate in an area where there is growing residential development and community viability. Ideally, the location should be one that is on the upside rather than the downside of the development curve. Communities go through a process of development, reach a peak, and then enter a period of decline. If the area has reached its peak and is entering the decline stage, the church will be coming on the scene after the time of major growth. This will make it more difficult for the church to experience rapid growth and have a long and vital ministry there. Usually, a church should try to find a location where they will be able to participate in the major growth cycle.

2) Visibility

Another key concern in selecting a location is good visibility. Church facilities should be located so they will be visible to a large number of people on their normal travel routes during the week. Jesus' words about "a city set on a hill" (Matt. 5:14, KJV) could be applied to an appropriate location for a church. Not all locations will put the church on a hill, but a good location will include significant visibility. Church facilities should be in the public view. Good visibility makes it possible for the church to make a statement to the community through its facilities. Beautiful landscaping, attractive buildings, and an appealing layout can all be a silent witness to those who pass. Having a highly visible site enables a church also to emphasize its ministry through program activities. Traffic around the church facilities can be a continual reminder to the community that the church is alive and effectively at work.

3) Accessibility

Church facilities should not only be visible they should also be accessible. In some instances, accessibility is more important than high visibility. Most of us have had the experience of trying to find a building we could see but could not easily reach. After several efforts to get to the building, we experienced considerable frustration. Some church sites are like that. They are visible from an interstate, but to reach the site one must travel a circuitous route that is difficult for newcomers to follow. A new church in Tennessee seeking property found a beautiful site with visibility from an interstate. It seemed an ideal location and the committee was immediately interested in purchasing it. However, a consultant pointed out that the only access to the property was through an industrial section that was an eyesore to the entire area. Wisely, the committee decided to look elsewhere.

Property located on divided highways can sometimes present significant problems of access for traffic crossing the median. If people must travel miles beyond the site to cross the median and gain access to the church property, this can create negative feelings. It will affect not only those coming to church from the opposite side of the median but also those leaving church and needing to cross the median to return home. Convenient access is a valuable asset to churches. In most instances, property that will restrict access and be a problem in attracting new members should not be selected for a church site. Restricted access may not be a real concern to committed church members, but it can certainly be a negative factor in reaching new people.

4) Capability

A good church site is one that has real capability for development and does not create severe limitations to the process. A number of conditions can limit development:

- Odd property shapes
- Long, narrow sites
- Severely sloping terrain
- Limited frontage for entrance and exit
- Problem subsoil conditions
- Easements and severe setbacks

An odd shape, such as a triangle, can be difficult to deal with because the sharp angles limit good utilization. Long, narrow sites, with the narrow side fronting on the road, create a nightmare because of the following:

a) The first unit often must be located toward the back of property, creating visibility problems. A new church needs significant exposure to the community and the first unit should provide this.

b) Parking often must be located inconveniently at one end of the property because the property width is not adequate for drives, buildings, and parking.

c) Interior circulation is limited to a linear pattern up or down the length of the buildings. This may mean that in the future people will have to walk through first unit buildings that were not designed for a larger congregation.

d) Limited entrance and exit points for vehicles create major traffic problems for a growing church.

Severe slopes either require expensive cut-and-fill operations or create serious problems for handicapped access. Limited frontage can restrict the number of access and egress points and force these to be located on busy traffic arteries. Problem subsoil conditions can range all the way from heavy rock formations requiring expensive blasting, to unstable soil that requires either excavation and backfill or pilings for adequate foundation support. Easements can divide property and create significant barriers to future development. Severe setbacks can shrink the space available for buildings.

One new church was given a twenty-five-acre site that quickly became the pride of all the charter members. It was beautiful property with three acres in the valley and the remaining twenty-two acres up the side of a sizable peak. The upper boundary of the property was along the center of the peak. From that point one could see for miles. The members enjoyed climbing to the peak and looking out over hundreds of new homes being built in the area. They assumed, because they could see from that point, those in the community would be able to see the church buildings.

However, there were a few problems with the site. The only point of access to the property was in an area where a one-hundred-foot frontage touched the highway. Approaching that point from one direction, the view of the property was completely obscured by the back side of the peak. Approaching from the other direction, there was only a very narrow corridor through which the property was visible and that point was forty feet or so above the valley setting. That meant visibility for the site was severely restricted. People would have to drive onto the church property for a good view of the development. Preliminary master-planning studies indicated the church really had about four acres of usable property without getting into the costly operation of developing the hillside. Any development on the hillside would involve blasting through solid granite. Thus, the projected cost of site preparation for the property soared. Fortunately, about the time all this was discovered, a real-estate developer offered to buy the property at an attractive price.

5) Long-Term Suitability

The site must be adequate to meet long-term development goals. How much property does a church need? A church needs one acre for every 100 to 125 people it expects to reach. This rule of thumb assumes the site has no extreme length to width proportions, no odd angles, no severe setback requirements, no limiting easements, no wetlands, and no restrictive slopes. The rule allows for what is generally regarded as an average church program. Churches that want to develop recreational ministries or weekday schools need more property. With an average program, a church that wants to grow to 500 in attendance will need four to five acres. That size site will provide for adequate parking, buildings, and appropriate green space.

Actually, the rule of thumb cited above should be used only in general planning. It should not be applied arbitrarily to every situation. A much wiser approach to the question of site size is to examine each site carefully in the light of the following questions:

- Are there restrictive factors on this site: severe setbacks, easements, topography, shape of the property?
- Are there restrictive local codes that should be evaluated: land coverage allocation, buffer requirements, water retention, or environmental impact?
- Will the church want to provide special ministries such as recreation or a weekday school?
- What plan will be followed in the development of facilities—campus or multilevel building plan?

The church that seriously evaluates each potential site by dealing with all these issues will be able to make a much more intelligent decision about the property being considered.

Perhaps something should be said about the minimum size for a church site. A good rule of thumb is two acres. That will provide space for 200 to 250 in attendance. To start a church with less than two acres seems to be shortsighted. Surely, most churches will have a vision of growth to at least this point in attendance. However, there are some situations in which even this rule of thumb must be laid aside. The cost of property in some metropolitan areas is such that some churches cannot afford two acres. They can purchase an acre located adjacent to adequate parking, work out a long-term parking arrangement, and use their acre primarily for buildings and a few handicapped parking spaces.

This is not an ideal arrangement, but it may be the only solution available at the moment. One of the big problems with this is that parking arrangements (unless they are in the form of a legally binding lease) can be changed almost overnight. Property may be sold and the agreement repudiated. The best choice is for the church to own sufficient property for parking, but that is not always an option.

Suggestions for Securing Adequate Property

If a church is unable to secure adequate property in the initial purchase, they should consider several other possibilities for providing for future property needs:

• A church might secure an option on connecting property they could purchase later. This would ensure the property would be available to them until the option expired.

• Several businessmen in the church might form a partnership and purchase additional property with the agreement to hold it for the church. They can regard this both as a business venture and as a means of helping their church.

• If a residence is located on the property the church is interested in and an older person owns it, the church may consider an agreement to purchase the property and allow the person to have a lifetime right to reside in the house. Of course, this can be an obstacle if the person lives so long that the growth of the church is stymied because the property is not available when needed. However, this agreement does ensure the church will eventually get the property. That may not always be possible if the church waits until the person dies to secure the property.

Many committees do not know how to search for available property. They are inclined to look only at property that is on the market. That is a mistake, for some of the best locations may not be listed for sale. A thorough search for property will take the committee not only to realtors but also to the tax books to find who owns a piece of property. The committee's first inquiry may be met with a rebuff. The owner may not seem interested in selling. If that is communicated rather emphatically, the committee may have to look elsewhere. But that does not mean the committee may not come back for future discussion with the owner. Sometimes, if a committee is convinced a site is ideal and desperately needed by the church, they can appeal to the owner's sense of investment in a worthy cause. Some owners will listen seriously if they are convinced their property really could make a significant contribution to the effectiveness of a church. When the negotiations are supported by faithful prayers they often produce fruit.

Frequently, a site in which a church is interested is much too large for the church's needs. With wise leadership a church can sometimes purchase the entire tract and then sell what they do not need. If a church considers this course of action, it should be prepared for unexpected developments requiring it to hold the extra property longer than expected.

A church near a military installation had an opportunity to buy seventeen acres with over six hundred feet of frontage on a four-lane boulevard. They were not financially able to buy the property and needed only five acres. Some strong leaders in the church helped put together a financial arrangement enabling the church to purchase the site. They expected to sell at least ten acres and had several companies interested in the acreage even before the deal on the property was closed. Within six months, the church expected to complete the sale and be out from under the excessive debt on the property. However, by the time it closed on the initial purchase, an economic slowdown had set in. The businesses interested in the extra property cut back on their expansion plans and delayed property acquisition. As a result, the church had to hold the seventeen acres for two or three years. The church could not have made it without outside help. Eventually, it sold the extra property and retained five choice acres for its building. This enabled the church to locate on the four-lane boulevard with excellent visibility and accessibility, and growth followed at an encouraging rate.

Critical Issues in Selecting A Site

1) Zoning

Local zoning should allow for church development on the site. Sometimes a church makes the mistake of assuming there will be no problem getting zoning changed to permit church construction. In some areas it may be relatively easy, but in others it is extremely difficult. The best rule to follow is not to purchase the property until the zoning issue has been resolved. The church may give a contract to purchase the property contingent upon the zoning change, but it should not close the deal and hope zoning can be changed.

2) Setback Requirements

Another real problem, especially on small sites, can be setback requirements. For example, a church in New Jersey purchased two acres with the intention of developing to a congregation of three hundred. Then, in the planning process, it discovered front and side setbacks of seventy-five feet and back and side setbacks of fifty feet. (See fig. 1.) The setbacks actually reduced the size of the property available for building to seven-tenths of an acre. In most instances, parking is allowed on the setback area. However, codes relating to green space must be met, and sometimes this eliminates paved parking on setback space. Committees are advised to thoroughly research these restrictions and know precisely what they are. They should not depend on hearsay or secondhand information.

3) Easements

Easements must also be dealt with in evaluating a site, and these are not always readily apparent. A high-voltage power-line easement can be quickly seen, but a sewer or gas-line easement may go completely unnoticed. Sometimes one must do a title search to discover easements on a piece of property. Research and study are required. If there is not time for this research, the church should request a contract with a contingent clause to cover unacceptable easements. This will relieve the pressure to tie up the property for the church. Some easements can be relocated, but power lines, gas lines, and sewer lines present real problems. Obtaining permission to relocate these lines often is a tedious process and the cost of relocation can be very high. These costs are paid by the property owner and not by the utility. If the property is acceptable only after relocating the easements, that should become a contingent clause in the contract to purchase.

4) Soil Tests

Soil tests should also be a part of the preliminary studies a church makes before purchasing a site. These tests can indicate soil conditions that will affect building foundations. Tests may indicate whether the builder will have to sink pilings to give adequate foundation support. They may show the presence of rock formations that will require expensive blasting. They can verify the capacity of the site to accommodate septic systems if a sewer is not available. Committees must understand that what they see is not all they get. Sometimes they get costly underground problems to work around.

5) Environmental Issues

Environmental impact studies are now required in many areas before building permits will be issued. These studies may involve water retention, traffic control, visual impact, tree and vegetation removal, wetlands classification, and other environmental issues. Water retention is one of the basic concerns. The question of how developments on the property will affect water runoff to adjacent property is a pressing concern. Many localities now require property owners to build water retention areas on their land to contain water runoff for a certain period of time.

Traffic control is often the subject of serious study. What effect

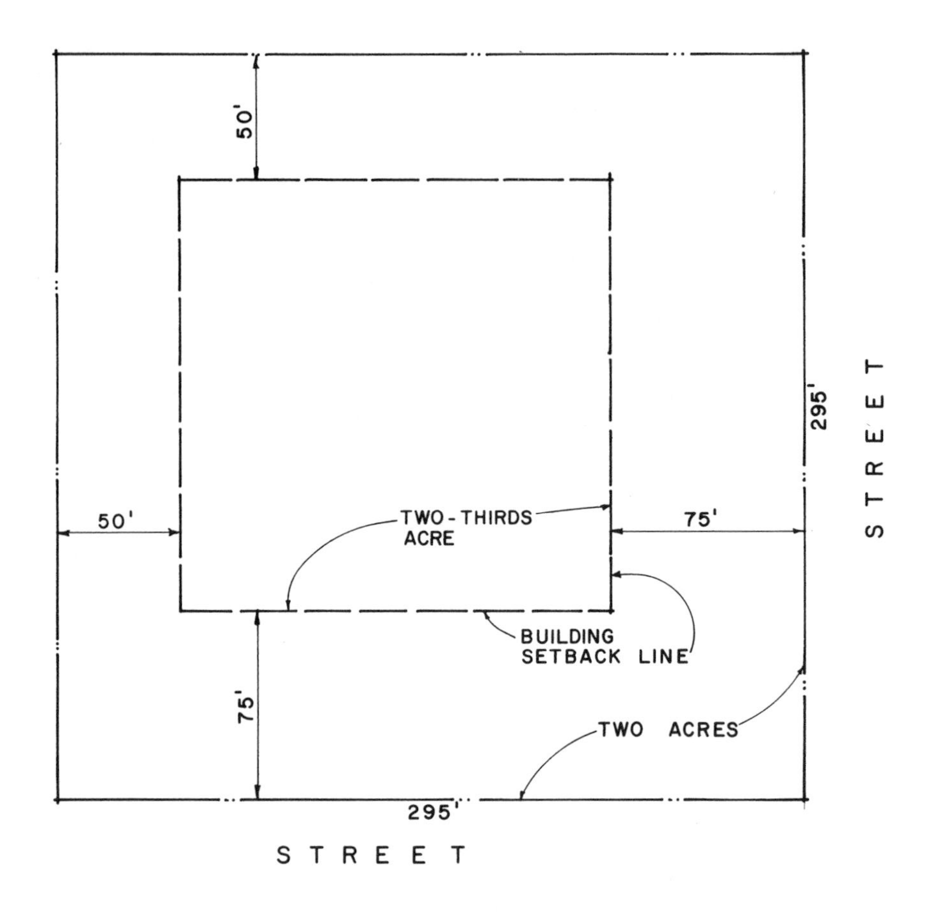

FIGURE 1: SITE REDUCED BY SETBACKS

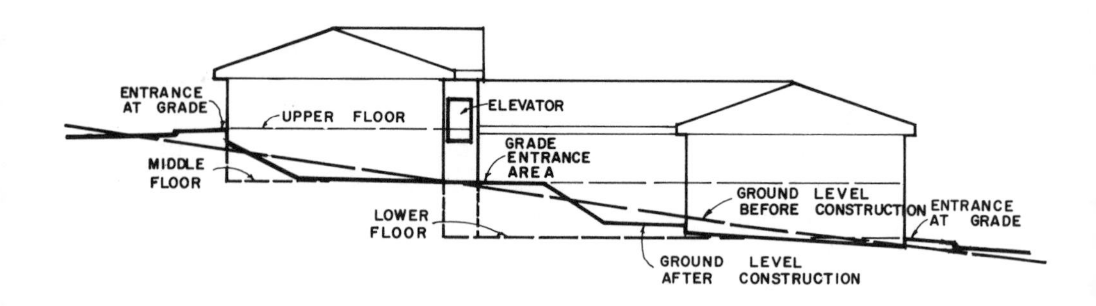

FIGURE 2: STEPPING A BUILDING DOWN A SLOPE

will church traffic have on existing traffic flow in the area? One church in a residential area with only two-lane streets sought approval to build a six-thousand-seat worship center. They had adequate property for parking. However, the issue of traffic control quickly became explosive in that community. How could the residential streets handle the extra traffic created by six thousand worshipers? Visions of two to three thousand extra cars in the area on Sunday mornings created real anxiety for local residents. The city fathers quickly became involved and blocked the church's plans for expansion.

In a growing number of situations the issue of visual impact is also being raised. Many communities have height restrictions for buildings. What kind of visual impact will developments on the property have on surrounding property? Sometimes planners float balloons at the height of projected buildings on the property for some idea of the visual impact of these structures.

Strict control of tree removal is now being enforced in some areas. Special permits are required to remove trees larger than a prescribed diameter. The same control is sometimes applied to certain protected plants and vegetation. Controls of this nature are expected to proliferate in the future so churches should anticipate this trend and prepare for it.

The preservation of wetlands is now mandated by local and federal laws. These areas may not have water standing on them at all times. They may be dry much of the time. However, if they are classified as wetlands, this seriously restricts how they can be used. Usually, owners are prohibited from any development on wetlands—building, paving, removing trees, or changing the natural terrain in any way.

6) Frontage

Street or highway frontage for the property is of critical concern. Adequate frontage is needed for safe access and egress. Entrances and exits should be planned with care to avoid creating dangerous traffic conditions in the area. There should be adequate sight distances in each direction to allow church traffic to slow and enter the property and to exit the property and enter lanes of moving traffic. A hill or a curve close to access and egress points can block the view of approaching vehicles and create hazards. Ideally, both church traffic and passing traffic should be provided adequate sight distances for safe vehicular movement.

7) Topography

The degree and direction of slope on the property can be a significant factor in development. Severe slopes create challenges for designers. Moderate slopes can sometimes be used to provide ground-level entrances at both floors of a two-story building. In other instances, designers can step a building up a slope and avoid excessive excavation (see fig. 2). However, even when ground-level entrances can be provided at different floors, planners should remember the need for interior accessibility. The ground-level entrances should not negate plans for elevators.

Radical slopes on property may make it virtually useless for church development. When considering a site for purchase, a committee should not depend on an "eyeball estimate" of the degree of slope. A topographical survey may be a wise investment to determine the property's conduciveness for church development.

8) Utility Connections

The committee should research utility connections. Are water, sewer, and electrical connections available within a reasonable distance? Sewer may be the most critical of all. If a church has to provide a sewer pumping station or its own sewer facilities there may be enormous costs involved. The costs of running utility service lines significant distances can also be a factor for a church. A thorough investigation should be made before purchasing the property. Discover not only whether a sewer connection is available but whether or not a pumping station will be required to tie into it. And don't rely on hearsay. Get the facts.

Master-Site Planning

Following the property purchase, the committee should seek help in preparing a comprehensive plan for its development. Unfortunately, many committees do not realize the importance of this prior to constructing the first building. For example, a church purchases ten acres of property and plans to build a first unit for 150 people. Committee members feel they have plenty of property and the location of the first building is not a critical issue. In truth, however, the best time to do master planning is when there is a clean slate: no buildings or paved parking to influence the development. This is the ideal time to develop a plan that makes the most of the site—a plan that magnifies the positive advantages and minimizes the negative aspects of the property. Note the following advantages of developing a master plan.

1) Master Planning Involves Extensive Study

Developing a master plan involves an extensive study of church programs, plans for outreach and ministry, buildings needed, and property selected. This study deals with the development and articulation of the church's dream and its translation into property and space requirements. It leads the committee to evaluate and prioritize program and ministry needs.

Master planning brings together the complex issues that touch the mission and work of the church, the potential for development and utilization of the property, the design and construction of church buildings, and the timely development of facilities to match the capability and needs of the church. The master plan evolves from the surveys and studies of the church and community, the dreams of the church, the growth-ministry strategy, and the vision and expertise of the professional planner.

Churches of all sizes profit from master planning. Failure to do adequate master planning can be critical and costly. The church with too little property to meet realistic growth projections and little prospect of securing additional property desperately needs a good master plan for maximum utilization of the site. The church that is growing rapidly needs the guidance of master planning so that developing facilities will be designed to sustain that growth. The church with excellent potential to become a large church needs special assistance so that short-term facility development will mesh with long-term needs.

The need for master planning is not limited to new congregations or to churches that are relocating. Churches in all stages of

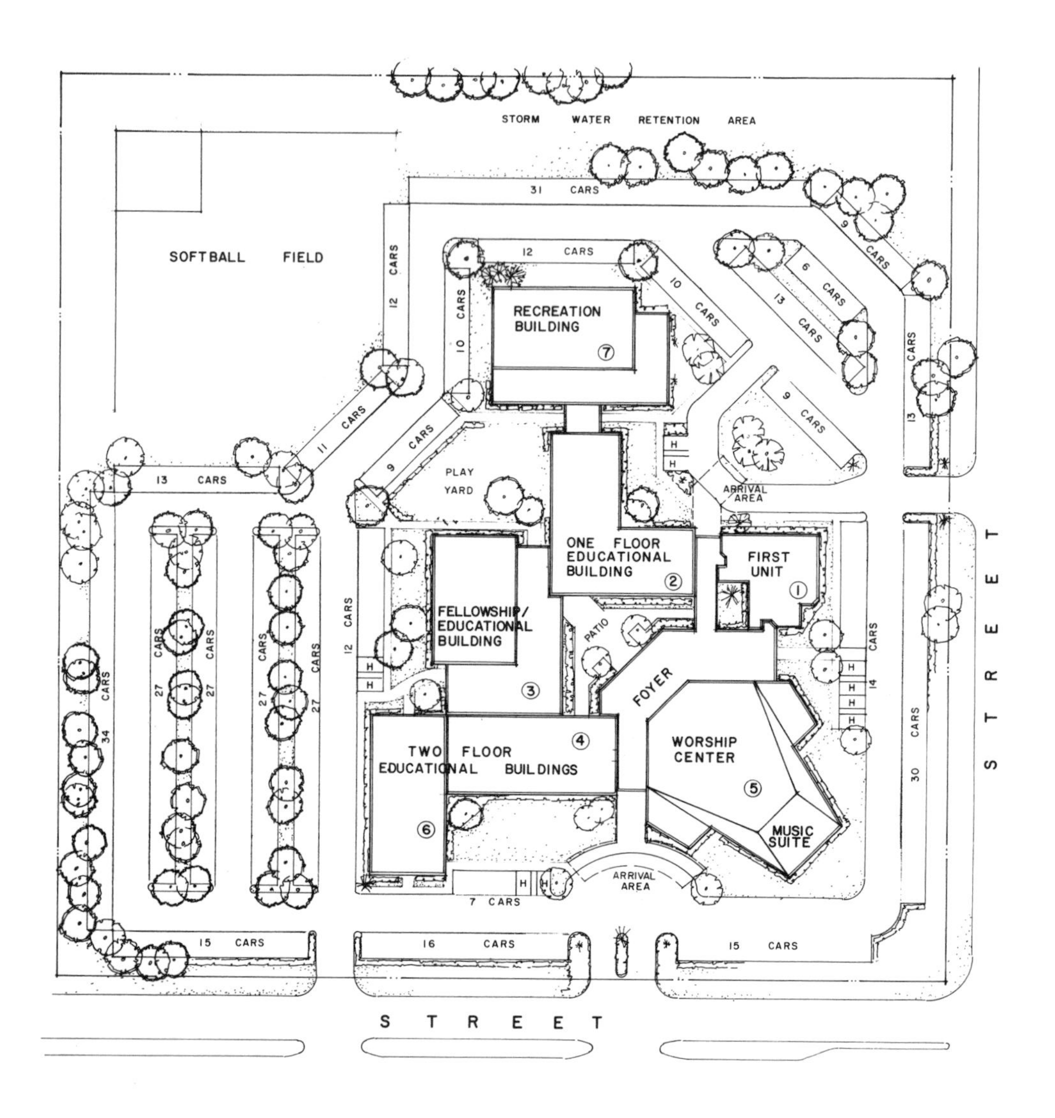

MASTER PLOT PLAN

PHASE	CAPACITY WORSHIP	CAPACITY EDUCATION	APPROX. BUILDING AREA	COMMENTS
1	138	138	3,750	PLAN S – 138
2	275	275	8,400	TWO WORSHIP SERVICES MAY BE BUILT IN TWO UNITS
3	500	500	10,400	INTERIM WORSHIP AND EDUCATION / FELLOWSHIP HALL
4	800 ±	775	12,960	TWO WORSHIP SERVICES
5	750-1,000	775	24,000 ±	MAY BE BUILT WITH EXPANSION INTO BALCONY AND TRANSEPTS
6	1,000 ±	1,000 ±	12,400	
7	RECREATION BUILDING WITH HIGH SCHOOL GYMNASIUM		10,000	MAY BE BUILT AS THIRD PHASE AND USED FOR INTERIM WORSHIP

PARKING SPACES

STANDARD SPACES	9' x 18'	416
HANDICAPPED SPACES	14' x 18'	10
	TOTAL	426

MASTER SCHEDULE PLAN

development need a master plan. This may be more pronounced for older churches that have never engaged in this discipline. Lack of master planning may have brought them to a point where circulation routes are inadequate and even confusing. Failure to do long-range planning may have contributed to inefficient utilization of property. The committee may need help in deciding which properties adjacent to the church would be most beneficial for future growth and expansion. They may need to deal with the question of whether new traffic patterns in the area should lead them to relocate main entrances and reorient their development. These and related problems create an urgent need for master planning. In many instances, a capable master planner can help find ways out of the impasse which committee members never would have envisioned.

Wise master planning involves a professional whose training and experience give him expertise for this process. The professional planner can bring exceptional gifts and insights to the task. His dealings with churches with differing needs, programs, properties, and challenges give him a broad perspective.

2) Master Planning Gives a Pattern for Development

Think of the master plan as a pattern for development, a map for charting the course for the future. It is a means for dividing the church's dream into phases so the church can pace its development. The distance between present realities and future possibilities is sometimes so great the average member may be totally bewildered by the challenge. A phased master plan bridges the distance and shows the church how to reach its goal. Phasing is creating "bite-size" chunks of the dream. The new church with one hundred in Sunday School sees an attendance of two thousand within the next twenty years. The master plan is a process which fills in the details and shows multiple phases of construction that provide adequately for growth needs in each stage.

3) Master Planning Correlates Needs and Resources

Balancing needs and resources is a key to wise master planning. In each phase of the plan, the church must correlate needs and available resources at that particular point. If a church tries to provide for needs too far in advance, it will be frustrated by inadequate resources. Ten years from now the church may need space for eight hundred people, but the resources of one hundred members are not adequate now for such a building program. Therefore, the church should consider a plan similar to the following:

- The first phase provides space for two hundred in worship and Sunday School.
- The second phase provides space for four hundred in Sunday School and plans for two worship services.
- The third phase plans for interim worship space for five hundred and two Sunday Schools.
- The fourth phase develops space for eight hundred in Sunday School and plans for two worship services in the interim worship building when needed.
- The fifth phase provides space for eight hundred in worship.

The critical need at each phase is to provide space for growth in worship and education either with multiple services or enlarged facilities.

4) Master Planning Balances Needs in Each Phase of Development

The master plan must balance space needs for buildings, parking, and green space requirements during each phase of development. Parking requirements are consuming larger and larger proportions of property. Regulations require a certain percentage of the property be retained for green space; this influences the entire development. Keeping all these issues balanced in each phase requires vision, creativity, and advance planning.

5) Master Planning Unites Mission-Ministry-Buildings-Property

All of these concerns are woven into the planning process. Mission and ministry are the driving issues and buildings and property become a part of the church's answer to these issues.

Remembering this helps keep planning priorities in line. Property and facilities are not the primary concern of the church, but are important only as they are tied effectively to mission and ministry.

6) Master Planning Allows for Adaptation and Change

The best plans may need to be adjusted in light of future developments. Therefore, the master plan is never set in concrete. It must be firm enough to provide guidance and direction, yet flexible enough to allow for modification to changing conditions and circumstances. The plan should be adaptable to enlargement or downsizing as needed. The sequence of phases should be changeable as circumstances dictate.

A master plan should not be developed and then blindly followed for the next twenty years. It should be carefully studied and reevaluated prior to each phase of construction. New developments or information should be brought into this evaluation. Over time, the church should have an improved perception of trends and conditions that could be only remotely perceived when the master plan was originally developed. Therefore, the plan will need to be updated and refined to meet developing needs.

Traffic Flow and Parking

People today depend on their automobiles so much that churches are forced to provide adequate off-street parking space. Local codes often require a ratio of one parking space for every three seats in the worship center. Parking consumes considerably more property than most people expect. One acre will generally provide parking for 110 to 120 cars. If a ratio of one parking space to every three seats in the worship center is required, a church of six hundred members will need two acres for parking.

Characteristics of a congregation can change parking needs dramatically. Churches with a large number of single adults or senior adults will need more parking spaces. These two groups are more likely to come with only one person in the car. In calculating parking needs, the committee should determine the average number of passengers per car. The easiest method is to count the cars and divide this number into the attendance for that day. This count should be made for several Sundays during peak attendance season. The goal is to provide abundant parking, not just enough to meet code requirements. If people can't find a place to park they will not likely visit the church.

Another factor that will affect parking requirements is multiple services. Scheduling two Sunday Schools or two morning worship services will proportionately increase parking needs. Those attending early services may not have exited the parking lot before those attending the next service. Separating the services by fifteen or twenty minutes will not eliminate the problem. Usually, the only solution is to provide more parking. Often the added vehicular congestion created by multiple services requires that driveways and passenger loading and unloading areas be expanded.

Entrances and Exits

Churches have a high volume of traffic arriving and leaving within a short span of time. This creates the need for well-planned entrances and exits so the traffic will flow at an acceptable rate. Exits should be spaced so exiting traffic will not block the flow from nearby exits. Generally, exits to the street should not be within one hundred feet of other exits. If possible, exits into more than one street should be designed to speed traffic flow. Traffic should be routed to avoid left turns across lanes moving in the opposite direction. Traffic will flow much faster if it exits only into the traffic lane immediately accessed at the exit.

Adequate exits should be planned in keeping with the capacity of the parking area. One church planning a worship center for fourteen hundred had only one exit from the parking lot. A consultant quickly pointed out that this would create enormous traffic problems. Imagine five hundred cars trying to exit onto a busy street from only one point.

Situate Parking Around the Building

Ideally, parking should be located all around the building and not clustered in one specific area. Many churches are interested in having a significant amount of parking on the front of the property so those who pass will see evidence of activity. This is a good idea if the parking area is well-designed with attractive landscaping. Increasingly, local codes require at least a minimum amount of landscaping in all parking areas. This helps provide appropriate screening and also creates an attractive and inviting atmosphere.

Handicapped Parking

Codes require handicapped parking spaces according to a mandated ratio that is adjusted as parking capacity increases. In some instances these spaces must be within one hundred feet of the entrance. Local codes should be checked for spacing and other requirements.

Arrival Shelters

One or more areas should be provided where passengers unload with sheltered access to the buildings. These should be designed for one-way traffic so passengers can exit on the side next to the building entrance. The sheltered area should be large enough to cover an entire car. The height must be carefully planned so it is adequate for vehicles but not so high that a blowing rain will sweep across the entire area. In some instances, a wall or plantings can screen this area and prevent excessive wind intrusion.

Arrival shelters should never be constructed between two buildings any closer than thirty feet apart. In fact, driveways between buildings so situated should be discouraged for safety reasons. There is always the chance that a child will dart out a door into the path of moving traffic. Every effort should be made to avoid locating a driveway that will cross any point of significant pedestrian traffic flow.

Passenger Loading and Unloading Areas

Other areas close to a main entrance should be provided for passenger loading and unloading. These are needed to accommodate:

- The elderly
- Those with small children
- Those who have difficulty walking considerable distances
- Those carrying boxes of supplies or instructional media

These areas should be designed so as not to block other traffic during the loading or unloading process. They should be located so passengers being discharged will not have to cross vehicular traffic lanes before entering the building.

Layout of Parking Lots

Parking lots should be designed by professionals who understand the importance of adequate spacing, driveway width, traffic flow, and landscape provisions. In many areas, codes address most of these concerns. Even if codes do not establish requirements, a church should plan its parking area with great care. Usually, the most efficient design is one that provides for 90-degree angle parking. Figures 3 and 4 indicate this layout requires 279 square feet per car. (This involves the parking space plus one-half the drive area behind it—a total of 9 feet by 31 feet.) Driveways should be designed to serve a row of cars on each side. If only one row of cars were served by the drive, each standard-size car in figure 3 would require 396 feet.

Some people find parking at 45 or 60-degree angles is faster and easier than at 90 degrees. (see figs. 4-6.) Drivers sometimes have to stop and back up to park at 90 degrees, and this slows traffic flow. Each parking lot should be carefully studied to determine the most efficient and functional layout for the area. Sometimes limited dimensions will indicate which parking angle will best utilize space. Parking lots designed for 45 or 60-degree parking may function better with one-way drives. These should be clearly marked and designed so a driver can move to any vacant space without having to exit the lot. Having to reenter the street in order to circle the lot adds to the congestion and creates additional hazards. One-way traffic patterns will usually function better if two-way entrances and exits are provided from the street because most of the traffic arrives and leaves in a short span of time.

Compact Car Parking

In many situations, smaller spaces will be provided for compact cars. (see figs. 3-6.) Some codes allow up to 30 percent of the spaces to be sized for compacts. Codes allow the minimum dimensions of these spaces to be seven and one-half feet (eight

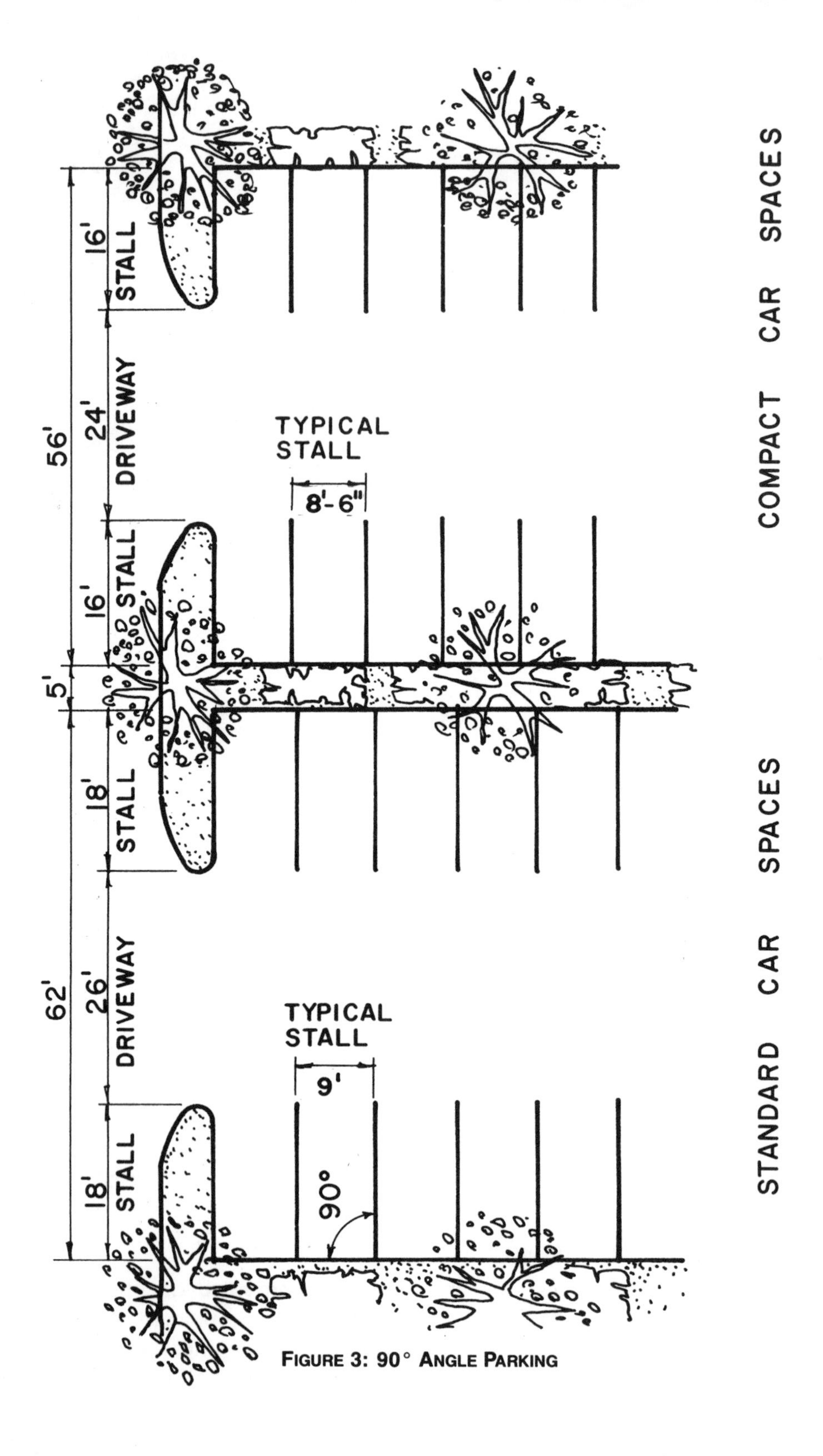

FIGURE 3: 90° ANGLE PARKING

PAVED AREA PER CAR		
	PARKING ONE SIDE OF DRIVE	PARKING BOTH SIDES OF DRIVE
STANDARD	379 SQ. FT.	290 SQ. FT.
COMPACT	324 SQ. FT.	252 SQ. FT.

TOTAL SQUARE FOOTAGE FOR 45° ANGLE PARKING

PAVED AREA PER CAR		
	PARKING ONE SIDE OF DRIVE	PARKING BOTH SIDES OF DRIVE
STANDARD	396 SQ. FT.	279 SQ. FT.
COMPACT	340 SQ. FT.	238 SQ. FT.

NOTE: AREAS OF ENTRANCE DRIVES AND ISLANDS NOT INCLUDED IN ABOVE TABLES

TOTAL SQUARE FOOTAGE FOR 90° ANGLE PARKING

FIGURE 4

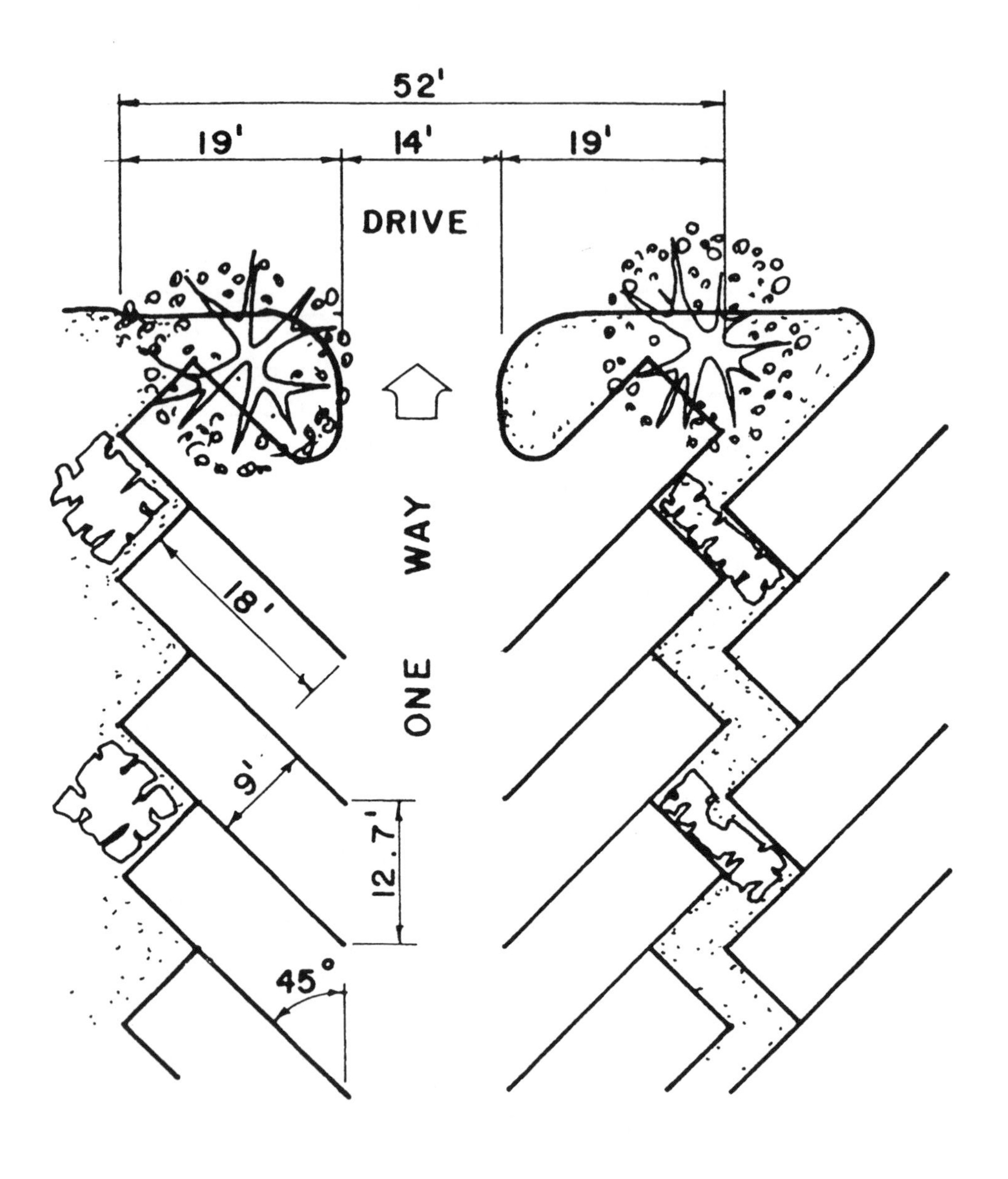

FIGURE 5: 45° ANGLE PARKING STANDARD CARS

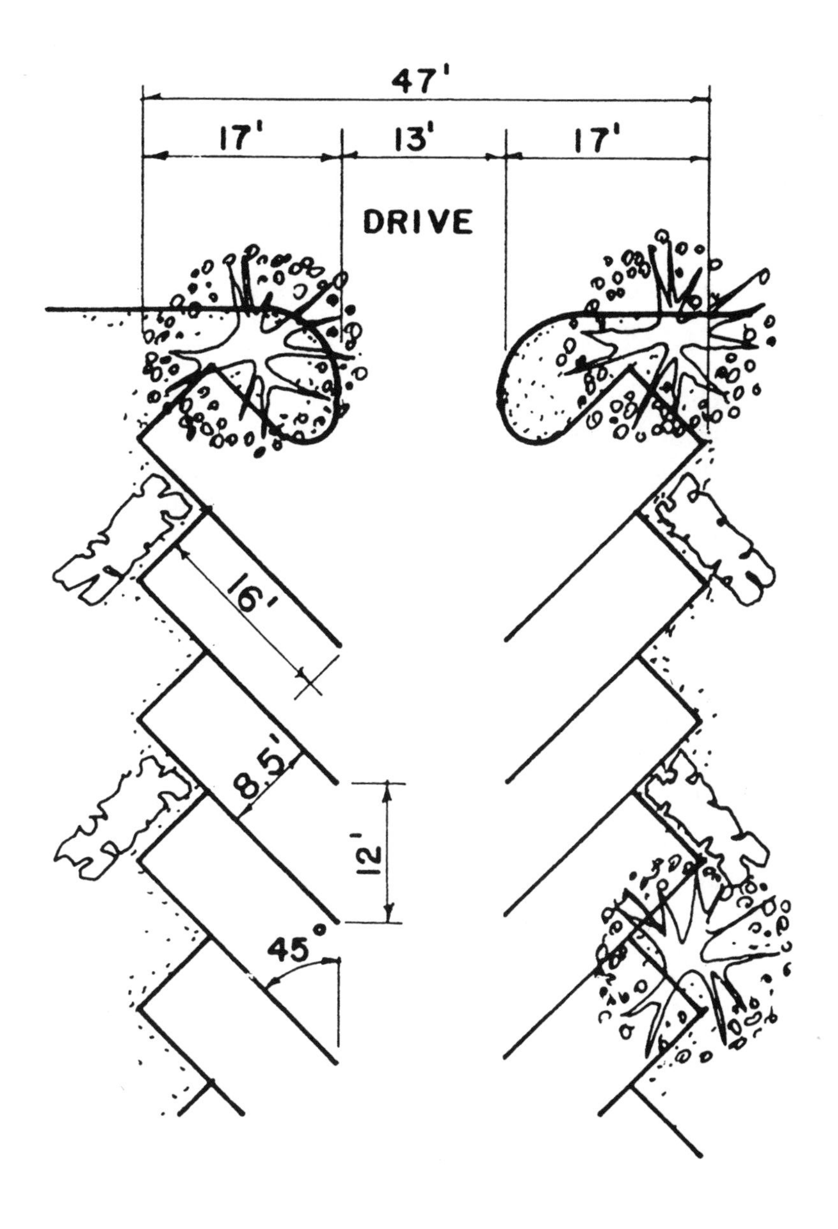

FIGURE 6: 45° ANGLE PARKING COMPACT CARS

and one-half feet is better) by sixteen feet. However, providing only minimum dimensions for compact spaces will not be acceptable to many congregations. The spaces should not be so small passengers will have difficulty loading or unloading. Designing adequate compact spaces can increase the capacity of the lot by as much as 10 percent. Group the spaces in sections so that they can be identified clearly. Locating the spaces indiscriminately around the parking lot will be confusing and will lead to misuse.

Landscaping

A church should not wait until the building is completed, parking lots and walkways paved, and exterior lighting installed to consider a landscaping plan. In fact, master-site planning will address all these issues and provide adequately for them in the early stages of the planning process. Creative landscaping can enhance building design. It can bring harmony to otherwise distracting architectural features. It can highlight major entrances and facilitate traffic flow. Planting islands can help direct traffic and define parking areas. Landscaping is a valuable asset for developing energy-efficient designs. (Using landscaping to facilitate energy conservation is discussed in ch. 8.)

Appealing landscaping can be the means by which a church touches people for the first time. Attractive, well-designed buildings and grounds offer people an inviting and appealing scene. They suggest the church's interest and concern for the community at large. Conversely, inadequate landscaping and unkept grounds can have a negative influence on people. They can suggest the church does not care about itself or others.

Well-designed landscaping is both attractive and functional. It should be planned in harmony with the architectural style of the buildings. Plant materials have character and should be selected so they are compatible with building style.

Walkways

Paved walks connecting parking areas and buildings are extremely important. They should be carefully designed to conform to normal paths of pedestrian traffic and be wide enough to accommodate anticipated traffic. To assist the visually impaired, surface material for the walk should be changed where the walk crosses a driveway. Large, paved areas near major entrances should be designed to provide space for gathering before and after services. Plantings around these spaces and the walkways can enhance their appearance and utility. The surfaces for these areas should provide safe footing—avoid slick, smooth surfaces or materials that become slippery when wet. Brick or stone surfaces that complement the materials used in the buildings can be very attractive.

Site Screening

Plantings can be used to screen unattractive surroundings and to frame the church property. They can also provide additional privacy for neighbors whose property is adjacent to the church. In many communities codes now require buffer screening for churches. Even if it is not required by local codes, screening is a thoughtful gesture churches can make to their neighbors.

Planting Suggestions

- Select slow-growing plants that require minimum trimming.
- Use plants that do well in the climate and require a minimum of special care.
- Use ground cover plantings rather than grass in small or isolated areas.
- Use masses of a few kinds of plants rather than a wide assortment.
- Avoid isolated plants in lawn areas.
- A mowing strip between shrubbery beds and lawn areas will reduce maintenance time (see fig. 7).
- Properly install plant material and apply mulch to retain soil moisture and retard weed growth.
- Select plants whose natural growth form is best suited to the overall design.
- If color is desired, flowering shrubs and trees will provide it and require less care than flower beds.

Lighting

Well-planned lighting can emphasize architectural features and landscaping and give the church significant visibility at night.

Lighting is also important for security. Parking areas, walkways, and entrances should be well-lighted, using a variety of light sources. Parking lots are usually lit with pole-mounted fixtures that spread light over the entire area. Adequate illumination is necessary to help reduce security problems. Walkways and steps can be lighted with either low mushroom-type fixtures installed at the sides of steps or louvered lights in walls along the edge of walks.

More interesting lighting can be designed if large trees are available. Fixtures can be placed twenty to twenty-five feet up in the trees and directed onto the area needing light. An alternate method is to place fixtures around the base of the tree and focus the lighting into the tree so it is reflected into the area. Both these methods of tree lighting have a soft moonlight quality that pro-

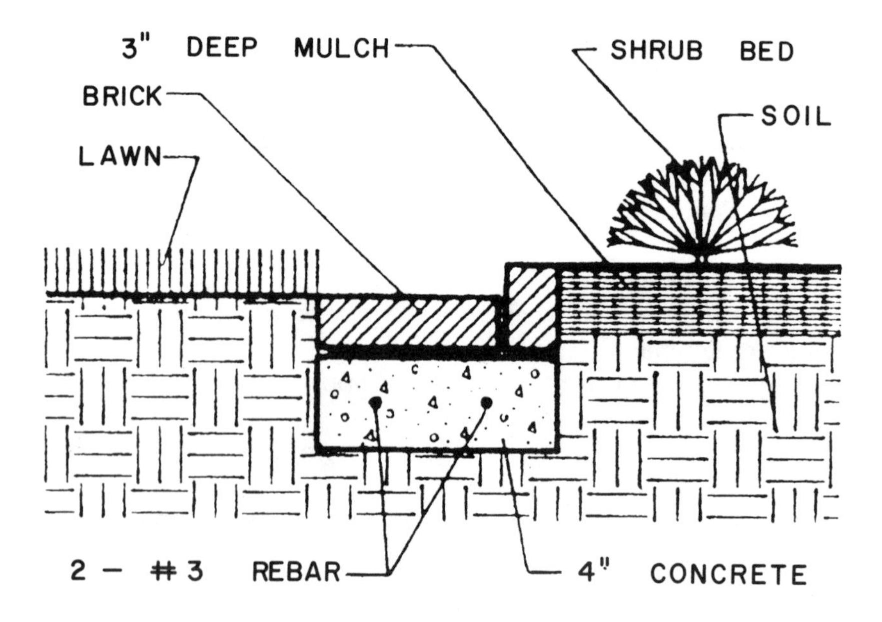

FIGURE 7: BRICK MOWING STRIP

vides illumination without creating harsh light, which might be offensive to neighbors.

Photoelectric cells and timers can be used to control the hours of operation for the lighting. These devices conserve electricity and extend the life of the lamps.

Churches that cannot afford to install exterior lighting systems as a part of the building project should install an adequate conduit so the systems can be added later at minimum expense. This will avoid additional installation costs which might be incurred if a basic conduit were not in place. It will also keep open the possibility of using the design as originally planned.

Signage

Attractive and adequate exterior signs are an asset to a church. They should be designed to complement the architectural style of the building. In *Designing Educational Buildings*, Charles Businaro makes the point:

> If the building is traditional, the style of signs might echo some of the shapes used for the building, such as an arch or trim detail. If the building is contemporary, a simplified design might be more appropriate. Whatever the style, the materials used for the sign should either match those on the exterior of the building or relate pleasantly to it.[1]

Codes in many cities now have strict criteria for size and location of signs. Check with your local codes department before designing or installing a sign.

Signs will be needed for the following:

- To give the church name and schedule for services
- To indicate traffic flow and parking areas
- To give directions to the offices, welcome center, worship center, educational building, and fellowship hall
- To specify reserved parking for the handicapped and visitors

Frequently, churches make the mistake of cluttering signs with too much information. If the sign is intended primarily for passing motorists, limit the information. The message of the sign should be brief enough to be read at a passing glance. If the sign is intended primarily for pedestrians, more information may be included. The size and style of the lettering should be designed for easy reading from the maximum distance.

Signage should be carefully correlated with the landscaping design so plantings complement rather than compete with the signs. A good planting design will help conceal lighting sources at the signs.

Design Service Areas with Care

Thoughtful attention to the location and provision of service areas can be extremely helpful. Consider the following areas in your planning:

1. Kitchen and Food-Service Areas
   a. Provide for convenient delivery of paper goods and groceries
   b. Give attention to a plan for garbage and trash removal including provisions for washing garbage cans and screening the area
2. Maintenance and Fuel-Service Areas
   a. Provide for delivery by large trucks if oil or liquid petroleum gas are used for heating
   b. Provide good service accessibility to mechanical rooms and utility equipment
   c. Screen equipment located on the ground and provide security fencing for equipment susceptible to damage or posing a hazard to children playing in the area

Storage Building for Grounds Maintenance

Many churches will need a building on the property where they can store mowers and other equipment used to maintain the grounds. Under no circumstances should gas-powered equipment be stored in buildings where people meet. This violates fire codes and insurance company policies because it creates fire hazards. Sometimes churches combine a storage building with a garage for a bus or van. Usually, this type facility should be located at the back of the property or at least away from primary traffic areas. Plantings to provide appropriate screening for these buildings will contribute to an attractive site design.

Notes

1. Businaro, Charles. Uniting Elements of Design. In Robert N. Lowry (Comp.), *Designing Educational Buildings* (Nashville: Convention Press, 1990), 51.

5

Working with Financial Concerns

Financial plans for church building programs should be based on sound principles. Five principles serve as guidelines for discussion in this chapter.

1. *Missions, programs, and ministry needs take precedence over building investments.*—The church is more than a building. What the church is and does is immeasurably more important than where it meets for services.

2. *Resources needed for personnel receive priority over building expenditures.*—Capable leadership is much more critical to the church's health and well-being than facilities.

3. *New buildings usually need a broader base of support than present income can provide.*—Conduct a capital fund-raising program and gear up for lifting regular giving to a higher level.

4. *Plan to pay for a new building on the basis of present financial potential—not with anticipated income from projected growth.*—Sound planning keeps within the limits of existing resources. If growth comes as fast as expected, additional income can be used to accelerate payments. If growth does not come as fast as anticipated, the church must still be able to handle its indebtedness without crippling programs, ministries, and missions.

5. *Commit no more than 25 percent of undesignated income to debt retirement unless the church is in a strong growth cycle.*—If substantial growth is underway, a church may commit between 30 and 35 percent to debt payments. Exceeding the safe debt limit is extremely risky and can be debilitating to the life and work of the church.

One of the first questions members ask about a proposed

church building project is "How much will it cost?" The next question: "How will we pay for it?" Often the answers provoke comments about extremely high construction costs. Each generation is inclined to think these costs are completely out of control. But visionary church-building projects have never been available at bargain basement prices. Churches usually find that raising adequate money for a new building is a challenging task.

Two extreme responses are made by churches to the financial demands of a building program. One extreme is represented by the congregation that is overly cautious and conservative and waits so long to build that the opportunity for growth is lost. The opposite extreme is represented by the church that rushes and ends up with staggering debt that impairs its effectiveness for years to come.

Fortunately, these responses are not the only ones available to a congregation. Careful evaluation and wise financial planning can transform the financial monster in a building program into a friend and helper. Financial plans are good servants but terrible masters. If the plans are sound and fiscally responsible, they will be good servants. If the plans are based on faulty assumptions and flawed financial projections, they can enslave a church and create enormous financial burdens.

Determining the Financial Potential of the Church

Few, if any, churches have unlimited financial resources for new buildings. Most churches have to prioritize their "want" list with regard to buildings and facilities. The challenge is to do this and still keep the primary focus on the purpose and goal of the church. Building programs have a subtle way of diverting attention from this purpose. A church can become so caught up in the pursuit of a building that it mortgages its primary dream and purpose. Church leaders must be vigilant at this point. No building is worth the sacrifice of mission and purpose. Therefore, the church must find a way to keep mission and purpose central even during the building construction and financing.

One way to do this is through comprehensive, financial planning that balances building investments with mission commitment. The starting point for this planning is a careful analysis of the financial resources of the church. What financial resources can be committed to the building project? That question is often not even raised in the early stages of planning. A committee may be so intent on defining the kinds of facilities desired that they do not even think of the church's potential to construct them.

Focusing on needs and growth challenges is the proper emphasis in the initial stages of planning. No committee should make financial potential the determining factor in the planning process. In reality, financial potential will be determined to some degree by the needs, possibilities, and visions generated in the early planning. Therefore, beginning the planning process by focusing solely on the church's financial potential is a mistake.

However, pursuing the planning process without giving timely, adequate attention to financial potential is also a mistake. No matter how great the needs and how glowing the visions, a church must eventually deal with the issue of financial resources. One of the keys to a successful building program is focusing on the financial concerns at the proper time. Ideally, this should be done as soon as needs have been defined and goals are being established. Financial realities become a part of the overall plan.

In determining financial potential the committee will look carefully at several resources:

1. Cash Available

Many churches anticipate needs well in advance and accumulate a building fund, savings account, or reserve fund to be used for a new building. These funds may come from memorials, special offerings, budget surpluses, or monthly deposits from budget appropriations. Whatever their source, these funds can make a tremendous difference when the time arrives for building. In fact, they often make it possible for a church to build with much less financial strain than would otherwise be possible. Sometimes these funds are the deciding factor in implementing the building program. Without them, the building could not have been constructed at that time.

2. Church Budget Allocations

How much can be allocated from the church budget for the building project? If there are no appropriations in the present budget, how much can the next budget commit to this purpose? Churches can safely allocate from 25 to 35 percent of undesignated income to debt retirement. The precise percentage will depend on a number of factors:

a. *Economic conditions in the community.*—An economic downturn can restrict the percentage of budget available for a building and economic prosperity can increase the percentage.

b. *Rate of growth in the community and church.*—A no-growth situation signals a church to guard against committing more than 25 percent of budget to debt retirement. Conversely, a rapidly growing church can often handle debt payments of 30 to 35 percent of budget.

c. *The kind of facility being planned.*—If the new building is a vital part of the church's growth strategy, more of the annual budget can be allocated to indebtedness on the assumption that a healthy growth rate will be sustained. A new building that makes no contribution to growth should be funded at a lower percentage of budget. The latter is especially true if there is a good possibility the church will run out of growth space before the building debt is paid.

The rule of thumb about safely committing a percentage of budget to debt retirement can easily be misunderstood. That rule does not mean a church can suddenly assign 30 percent of its budget to debt retirement and not miss those funds. A sudden shift of this magnitude will have serious financial repercussions unless adequate preparations have been made. Imagine what would happen to your personal budget if you suddenly lost 30 percent of your income. The rule of thumb simply indicates, even with proper preparations a church can safely allocate no more than 25 to 35 percent of its undesignated income to long-term debt payments.

Preparations for this kind of allocation often involve raising the level of giving in the church so additional funds become available. In some instances, the pattern of budgeting will have to be restructured. Some budget items will have to be reduced to free adequate funds for loan payments. This raises the specter of reducing commitments to missions and ministries. Churches frequently have to struggle with this issue. Fortunately, many churches have demonstrated that new buildings can be constructed without siphoning off resources from missions and ministry. Members who think first about cutting mission gifts to pay for a building may already have lost their sense of mission.

3. Anticipated Income from a Capital-funding Program

Often the greatest untapped financial resource for church building is a capital fund-raising program. This program, led by a competent outside professional, can generate significant funds. The average church can raise about 1.7 times its annual income over a three-year period. Many churches actually raise more than that. This average means a church with a budget income of $200,000 could expect to raise about $340,000 in a capital-fund program.

These programs are so successful some churches use them to pay virtually the total cost of a new building. Usually, this involves several programs following in close sequence. Green Street Baptist Church in High Point, North Carolina, had four programs in thirteen years. Each one was successful and helped provide adequate facilities for relocation.[1] Details about planning capital-fund programs will be discussed later in this chapter.

4. Estimating Borrowing Potential

Most churches involved in significant building programs have to negotiate long-term loans. Seldom is a church in a position to pay cash for the building. The critical issue is how much long-term indebtedness can a church afford to incur without being overextended. Often this question is answered for the church by the institution making the loan. However, in some instances, institutions seem willing to lend more than a church can afford to borrow. Churches which issue bonds also have to deal with the possibility they may be able to sell more bonds than they can safely amortize.

There are several ways to calculate the safe borrowing potential of a church:

a. *On the basis of the value of property and buildings.* —Seventy-five percent of the appraised value of these holdings is often used as a criterion for establishing borrowing potential. According to this rule, a church with property valued at $500,000 could borrow up to $375,000.

b. *On the basis of budget funds available for amortizing a loan.*—The basic rule is that a church should commit no more than 25 to 35 percent of its undesignated income to loan payments. The total loan potential can be calculated once the annual budget appropriation is determined. For example, a church with a $200,000 income decides it can allocate only 25 percent of its income or $50,000 a year, to debt retirement. A fifteen-year loan at 11 percent interest requires annual payments of $136.44 per $1,000 borrowed. Divide $50,000 by $136.44 and the result is $366.46. Multiply that by $1,000 and this gives a total loan potential of $366,460.

c. *On the basis of a multiple of the total church budget.*—The multiple comes from a chart and is determined by the interest rate on the loan, the length of the loan, and the percentage of the budget the church can commit to debt retirement. For example, a church which can allocate 25 percent of its budget to debt payments on an 11 percent loan for fifteen years would use the multiple of 1.7. A budget of $200,000 multiplied by 1.7 would yield a safe debt potential of $340,000. (See the chart in fig. 8 for other multiples.)

In the examples just given, note the potential in (a) is $375,000; in (b) is $366,000, and in (c) is $340,000. The approach used in (b) is the most precise. The value of church property does not always indicate the present financial resources of the congregation. Using a multiple of the total church budget as in (c) is useful only for estimating purposes. In the final analysis the issues raised in (b) are the most critical in determining the parameters for borrowing potential.

The illustrations cited assume there are no other outstanding loans. If other debts exist, they should be included in the evaluation. For example, if the church can safely afford to borrow $366,000 and already has a $100,000 loan, the safe debt limit is reduced to $266,000. If the $100,000 loan will be retired in three

Using Budget to Project Safe Debt Limit				
% of Budget	10% Interest		12% Interest	
To Debt Retirement	15 Yrs.	20 Yrs.	15 Yrs.	20 Yrs.
35%	2.7	3	2.4	2.6
30%	2.3	2.6	2.1	2.3
25%	2	2.1	1.7	1.9
20%	1.5	1.7	1.4	1.5

Find appropriate factor and multiply church budget by factor. The result is the safe debt limit for a church using these guidelines.

Example: A church can secure a 10% loan for 15 years and can commit 30% of budget to debt retirement. The factor is 2.3 times budget. With a budget of $100,000 the safe debt limit is $230,000. Debt retirement payments would be $29,670 annually—just under 30% of budget.

FIGURE 8

years or so, the loan potential evaluation may be adjusted to reflect this.

There is the possibility of combining an existing loan with a new loan. However, in some situations this is not recommended. Two of these are: (a) when the existing loan has a much better interest rate than can be obtained on the new loan, and (b) when the points charged for the new loan result in significant additional cost if the existing loan is incorporated in the new loan. For example, if three points are being charged, adding an existing loan of $100,000 to a new loan would add a point charge of $3,000. The committee will need to determine if the extra cost is worth what is gained by consolidating the loans.

Planning a Budget for the Building Project

The average layperson thinks of the building budget almost exclusively in terms of actual construction costs. Such oversimplification often creates communication problems. Early discussion of cost centers primarily on construction. The committee may tell the church that the planned facility of 10,000 square feet will cost $500,000 based on the projected square footage cost. The estimate may be on target, but the church may be surprised to find the project will actually cost over $600,000. The extra $100,000 came from fees, furnishings, and other items the committee had not included in the early estimate. Experience teaches that these miscellaneous costs can add another 25 to 30 percent to the total cost of construction.

Most committees will need help planning a budget for the entire project. The following items should be included:

1. Land acquisition (if required for the project)
2. Projected cost of construction
3. Site development
   a. Grading, filling, and compaction
   b. Paving
      1) Curbs, gutter, and streets
      2) Sidewalks and parking
   c. Borings and soil tests
   d. Utility connections and lines
   e. Landscaping
4. Fees
   a. Architect
   b. Surveyor
   c. City impact
   d. Permits and inspections
   e. Consultants
   f. Insurance and bonding
   g. Legal
5. Furnishings and all equipment not in the general contract
6. Financing
   a. Construction loan
   b. Closing costs
7. Contingencies

Many of the items in the budget must be estimated because exact costs are not known when the budget is developed. There are, however, some fairly reliable estimates. Landscaping costs can equal 7 percent of construction costs. Furnishings costs can add another 10 to 15 percent to the total cost of construction.

Contingencies should be covered with an amount equal to 5 to 10 percent of construction costs. Fees can be equal to 15 percent of the cost of construction even if no city impact fees are involved.

If one uses even the low side of these rules of thumb, the total becomes very significant. One quickly sees how the total project cost could amount to over 30 percent more than the contract price for the building. Taking the time to do adequate budget planning for the project is extremely important. The more extensive the planning, the more likely the possibility of developing a realistic budget. A sample building project budget is found in appendix B.

Controlling the Cost of the Project

Sooner or later most committees face the painstaking task of trying to reduce or control building costs. Many budgeted items are beyond the control of the committee. But some costs will be directly determined by decisions of the committee. Broadly speaking, five basic factors determine the major costs of a building:

- Size of the building
- Design of the building
- Materials used in the building
- Labor involved in construction
- Financing costs

There are numerous other categories, but those noted above are the major ones. Usually, the ultimate cost of the project is determined more by these factors than by others.

These five factors can be adjusted and manipulated to influence final costs within certain parameters. For example, decreasing the size of the building is an effective way to bring costs to a manageable level. Adopting a simpler design, or using more economical building materials can significantly lower costs. Using volunteer labor—if this is an option—can reduce the cost on some projects by as much as 40 percent. However, the factor offering the greatest possibility of reduction of cost is financing. Frequently, churches pay more interest on long-term financing than the building itself costs.

Why don't church leaders recognize and explore this fact more often? Why do they fail to see the importance of adequate advance financial preparation for building programs? Leaders are often delinquent in their responsibilities during the period when the church could accumulate funds and utilize compounded interest to save thousands of dollars in financing costs. Then in the planning and building phases, they suddenly become cost-conscious and work frantically to trim construction costs. On a $500,000 project they may find ways to cut $50,000 to $75,000. Once those cuts are made, the committee often relapses into a state of fuzzy financial reasoning and adopts a plan that will force the church to pay hundreds of thousands of dollars in interest over the life of the loan.

Efforts at cost control should not focus on construction costs only. Such focus can result in mediocre design, use of inferior materials, and cheap buildings with high utility and maintenance costs. Of course, such efforts need not produce negative results. They can be a wise and valid part of cost control. However, committees should realize that the largest possible savings are usually in controlling financing costs. Remember, too, dollars saved in financing have no negative impact on the quality of the design or construction of the buildings. Conversely, money spent on financing does not buy more space, better design, or superior quality construction. All it buys is time to repay the loan. Therefore, churches would be wise to concentrate more on ways to control the cost of financing building projects.

The most obvious way to do this is by raising a significant amount of money prior to the building's completion. Reference has already been made to accumulating a building fund and to capital fund-raising as a means of achieving this goal. Another approach, often overlooked, is regular monthly transfers from the operating budget to the building fund. A church should begin this practice several years before the building is needed.

Assume, for example, that a church expects to launch a $500,000 building program within the next three years. There are no funds currently available for the project. The finance committee anticipates the needs and recommends: (1) that the church budget allocate $2,000 a month to a building fund, and (2) that the allocation be increased by $500 a month in each succeeding budget. If these funds are placed in an account drawing as much as 7½ percent interest, the building fund will contain $100,000 after three years.

Assume this church conducts a capital fund-raising campaign immediately and pledges twice its annual income of $182,000. Three years later the church will have $364,000 from capital funds and $100,000 in the building fund. If the building program were timed to be completed at that point, the church would be able to occupy the new building with a debt of less than $40,000. If the members extended their capital-fund pledges for four more months, the indebtedness would be completely liquidated. The church would have paid less than $10,000 interest for the total project.

Suppose this church had taken a different approach and borrowed $450,000 for fifteen years at 11 percent interest. The church would have paid $470,970 in interest for the fifteen-year loan. Of course, they could have occupied the new building twenty-seven months earlier than in the previous plan. However, the earlier occupancy would have cost them $17,072 a month. (This represents the difference in interest paid, $460,970, divided by the twenty-seven months.)

The point of these examples is to suggest churches begin financial preparation much earlier than usual. It is not to advocate that churches delay building programs until they have funds on hand to pay for the building. The examples give rather dramatic illustrations of how one church could have saved $460,000 in financing costs.

Of course, some churches do not have these options. Churches growing at a rapid rate often cannot wait three years for a new building. Other churches in times of high inflation may find building costs are escalating at a higher rate than the interest on their building fund. In those times, higher building costs can wipe out the effects of compounded interest. However, even during those times, churches are wise to raise as much money as possible prior to the time of construction.

One other point needs to be made about the example of the church that waited three years to build. If waiting caused the church to lose its growth impetus or slowed its evangelistic outreach, the money saved would have been a bad investment. Keep in mind the mission of the church is not to save money but to be vitally involved in the saving work of Christ. If the choice is between saving interest and reaching people for Christ, the decision must be for the latter. However, there is usually no reason why a choice must be made between these two alternatives. In many instances, a church can rent space, borrow space, secure temporary space, or begin dual services to provide growth space. A vital, creative church can usually find ways to continue growing during the time they are accumulating funds for a new building. But they must start early enough to be financially prepared when construction time arrives.

Utilizing Capital Fund-Raising

A capital fund program, led by a capable and experienced professional, can be a tremendous asset to a building program. It can bring a church together in a significant spirit of unity in pursuing the project. It can strengthen the church fellowship. It can dramatically illustrate the strengths and resources available in the church.

Capital-fund programs are developed on the basis of well-defined principles of fund-raising. These include:

- The importance of a well-developed and trained organization
- The essentials of adequate communication
- The principle of prior commitment—each person makes a commitment before appealing to others to respond
- The principle of sacrificial giving
- The principle of making a firm commitment

The initial campaign may extend over a period of three months and involves three phases: preparation and training, communication, and commitment. The program climaxes with individual and family pledges over and above regular offerings over a three-year period. The total pledged often exceeds the leaders' dreams. On an average, churches raise 1.7 times their regular annual income over the three-year period. Many churches have far exceeded that average, some raising as much as seven times their annual income.

The amount raised is usually related to the sense of priority the congregation feels about the proposed building. In most instances, the highest priority is given to a worship center. The next is given to educational space, followed closely by fellowship space. Recreation buildings are often regarded as lower priority projects. Efforts to pay off indebtedness usually receive the lowest priority.

Ideally, capital-fund programs should be scheduled at least two years before planned completion of the new building. The general rule is to schedule the program as early as possible so maximum funds are on hand when the building is finished. However, at least two issues must be resolved before programs can be successfully conducted. A church decision should be made about the kind of space to be constructed; and a front elevation or perspective of the proposed building should be available.

These two concerns are important because they help answer questions about the need for a new building and what the building will look like. Full details about the building need not be completed at this point, but people need enough information to motivate them to give. Imagine the lack of motivation in the appeal, "We do not know what we will build or what it will look like. We just want you to give sacrificially so we can construct some kind of building." Contrast that with a program that clearly states, "We want to build a worship center to seat six hundred because we have been in two worship services and are nearing capacity. This is the style building we plan to construct."

The economic benefit from the capital-fund program is often spectacular. Every dollar raised in the effort can save two dollars in interest and pay back over the life of a fifteen-year loan at 12 percent interest. Not only does the church save the interest, but it is also freed from the burden of long-term principal payments. Because the money is given early in the program, the church does not have to raise that amount later. Frequently, this frees a church to make productive investments in programs and ministries to keep the church growing. It also opens the way for a fast-growing church to prepare for the next building program which might have been delayed by long-term indebtedness.

Sometimes people ask how the capital-fund program affects regular giving. In many instances, budget gifts increase as a direct result of the program. One church experienced a 30 percent increase in regular giving immediately after a capital-fund campaign. Others have had similar responses. Of course, some churches have had a decline in budget giving following these programs, but the decline may not have come as a result of the program. It may have been the result of economic conditions or internal problems in the church. Successful capital-fund campaigns are a great asset not only to stewardship training but also to the total life of the church.

Following a successful program, one pastor said, "The money we raised in this campaign was only incidental to the great spiritual benefits we experienced." Another pastor exclaimed, "This is one of the greatest programs we have ever had in our church!"

Exploring Resources and Applying for a Loan

The availability of church loans for building is often closely related to the economy. When the economy is booming and money is available, most churches usually have no major problem securing a loan. During a credit crunch, lenders can be more selective and churches may get pushed aside. Banks, savings and loan associations, and church bonds are major sources of loans for church building programs. Other sources include insurance companies, trust companies, mortgage investment companies, and individuals.

One church involved in relocation obtained a $200,000 loan from one of the members. The terms provided that the first two years would be interest free to the church. After that period, the church would pay the prime rate on the loan. This generous arrangement allowed the church to negotiate an attractive loan package with a local bank for the additional funds needed.

Church bonds have been a popular and successful method of financing church construction. A church bond is a security instrument and, therefore, subject to certain state and federal security laws. Churches issuing bonds will need the services of an attorney and other professional guidance to enable them to conduct a sales program that meets security regulations. Leaders in the church need to be aware of the total cost of bond issues. In addition to the interest paid to bond holders, there may be sales costs and accounting costs. These additional costs may add 1 to 2 percent to the effective interest paid on the bond program. Therefore, a bond issue at 10 percent may actually cost the church 11 to 12 percent interest.

Another disadvantage with bonds is that the total issue is usually sold prior to the time construction begins. Interest begins as soon as the bonds are sold. This means the church pays interest on the entire bond issue even before the money is needed for construction. With a construction loan, the church pays interest only on the sum that is borrowed to pay construction bills.

Church bonds can be an attractive means of financing if the total costs to the church are less than the costs of a commercial loan. For a new church with no established financial rating, bonds may be the best avenue for financing. However, church members should recognize that a bond program is nothing more than a means of borrowing money. Bonds should not be confused with capital funding. Money raised with bonds must be repaid with interest. Money raised with capital funding is a gift to the church.

In recent years, some denominational agencies have expanded their church loan provisions. Some of these agencies also assist churches in putting together a loan and bond program when the church needs more than the agency can lend. For example, if a church needs $1,750,000, they might obtain a million-dollar loan commitment on the condition that they sell $750,000 in church bonds.

Some denominations have loan programs primarily for new churches. Grants are also available in some instances to be applied on the purchase of property and on new construction. Committees should check with their denominational leaders to see what help is available.

Before a church applies for a long-term loan, the committee should complete background financial studies and assemble the following:

1. A detailed financial statement
   a. Total assets, liabilities, and cash on hand
   b. A complete financial report for the past twelve months
   c. Annual reports for the past five years listing budget, budget offerings, and total gifts
2. A numerical growth record for the past five years
   a. Sunday School enrollment and average attendance
   b. Resident membership
   c. Number of adults in Sunday School
3. A community profile
   a. Total population
   b. Average age
   c. Median income
   d. Growth patterns
   e. Projected growth
4. Detailed building project budget
5. A set of preliminary drawings for the building. (Final approval of the loan will usually require detailed construction drawings, but application for the loan may be made before these are completed.)

Leaders who make the presentation to the lending institution should be selected with care. If possible, select leaders who deal with the institution on a routine basis in business or personal finance. These persons lend credibility and bring added skills in negotiation to the process. They should make a clear and convincing presentation that establishes the need for the building, the provisions the building will bring, and a sound plan for financing. If this plan follows the basic financial suggestions in this chapter, it will be seen as credible and responsible. The plan should reveal the fact that the committee has done adequate background studies, sound financial evaluations, and realistic projections for amortizing the proposed loan.

Remember, loan officers may not be impressed with statements about faith and prayer. The assertion that the church is trusting the Lord to open the way to do what seems impossible may not win any points for the loan application. Glowing statements about anticipated growth that are unsupported by data will not be convincing. Graphs and visuals charting growth will communicate much more effectively. Do not give the impression the church expects new people who may be reached to pay for the building. Rather, show how the church's present resources will be able to repay the loan.

Negotiations will also need to be made for a construction loan so the church can pay construction costs as they are billed. A construction loan amounts to a letter of credit allowing the church to draw funds as they are needed for the building project. Construction financing usually cannot be arranged until a long-term loan commitment has been made. The construction loan may be obtained from the institution providing the permanent financing or from another lending agency.

Committees should apply to a number of lending agencies, and then compare the terms and conditions that are offered. Not all agencies will offer their most favorable terms to churches. By shopping and thoroughly exploring the mortgage market, a committee can obtain the most attractive terms available in the area.

Developing the Financial Package

The financial package for a building program includes the following:

- Projected timetable for the implementation of the project
- Total cash that will be available when the loan is closed
- Anticipated income still to be received from capital-fund pledges
- Proceeds from the permanent loan or from the sale of bonds

The committee needs to know what the total project costs will be, what the total financial resources are, and the anticipated timetable for the project. With this information they can begin to put together the financial package. Timing is critical because it can add enormous financing costs. See the example given on page 72 as an illustration. Other examples showing packages with financing costs ranging from \$2,500 to \$470,000 are given in appendix B. These illustrations present convincing arguments for capital-fund programs and for developing a sound financial package that minimizes interest costs.

In putting the package together, special provisions must be made to cover capital fund income that will not be available at the time the loan is closed. For instance, if the capital-fund program is only half completed at the time of closing, approximately half of the amount pledged will need to be borrowed to cover income not yet received. Later, as the pledged amounts are received, they can be applied directly to the loan. This will reduce the principal more quickly and cut interest costs. The church should apply capital-fund money to the loan as soon as it is received and not use it to make regular, monthly loan payments. The pledged money should be used for accelerated payments which will quickly reduce the interest of the loan.

For example, assume a church enters a building program with a project budget of $500,000. They have $50,000 in a building fund and pledge $309,000 in a capital-fund program. This means that at the end of three years the church will have $359,000 plus interest. However, the church decides it cannot wait for three years for the new building. Construction is started, and the building is completed when only half of the amount pledged is in hand. Anticipating this, the committee arranged for a loan of $180,000 to cover the outstanding pledges plus $141,000 for the long-term debt. If the church makes monthly payments on the loan and also makes lump-sum payments as the capital fund pledges are paid, at the end of eighteen months the $180,000 for the outstanding pledges should be repaid. But, if the church uses the capital fund money just to make regular loan payments, much of the advantage of capital funding will be lost and thousands more in interest will have to be paid.

This example brings up the subject of accelerating payments. In most instances, the terms of a loan allow the borrower to make additional payments and speed the amortization process. This has a dramatic effect on lowering interest costs. The principle of accelerating payments is actually quite simple. Check the amortization table in figure 9 for an illustration. Suppose the treasurer is making payment number six and discovers sufficient funds are on hand to make an extra payment. The principal for payment number seven ($3,345.67) is paid, and the interest charge for that payment is canceled. Payment number eight will be due at

MORTGAGE AMORTIZATION TABLE

I MORTGAGE AMOUNT =======> $321,000
II INTEREST RATE ==========> 11
III NUMBER OF YEARS ========> 6
MONTHLY PAYMENTS ARE ======> $6,109.92

PYMNT.	PRINCIPAL	INTEREST	BALANCE
1	3167.42	2942.50	317,832.60
2	3196.45	2913.47	314,636.20
3	3225.76	2884.16	311,410.40
4	3255.32	2854.60	308,155.10
5	3285.17	2824.75	304,870.00
6	3315.28	2794.64	301,554.70
7	3345.67	2764.25	298,209.00
8	3376.34	2733.58	294,832.70
9	3407.29	2702.63	291,425.40
10	3438.52	2671.40	287,986.90
11	3470.04	2639.88	284,516.80
12	3501.85	2608.07	281,015.00

FIGURE 9

the regular time next month. There is no limit to the number of prepayments that can be made. Every prepayment of principal eliminates the interest attached to that payment and moves the borrower through the amortization schedule at an accelerated rate. The interest saved over the life of the loan can be significant.

Another possible package to consider is one that involves church bonds and a capital-fund campaign. These two programs are not used often together because of the following:

Both programs involve an extensive amount of congregational time and energy. The church involved in both programs will spend about six months in intense financial promotion. That is too heavy a concentration on financial issues for the average congregation.

Both programs use some of the same promotional principles and there is the possibility that overemphasis can reduce effectiveness.

Both programs are designed to raise significant sums of money from the church membership. This can place members whose financial resources are limited in a difficult position because they have to borrow the funds from a bank to purchase bonds. To ask members to give sacrificially to a building program and then a few months later ask them to borrow money to purchase church bonds can create unreasonable pressure. Of course, if members have available funds to purchase bonds the pressure is eliminated. Even so, it is still possible to weaken capital-fund giving by announcing a bond program. Some members may feel purchasing bonds is their financial contribution, and this represents the same dedication as capital-fund giving. Actually, the two programs are not even in the same ballpark. Buying a church bond is a financial investment, not an act of giving.

Churches deciding to have a capital-fund program and also sell bonds should communicate that decision clearly to the membership in the early days of planning. Members need to know this plan in advance. The capital-fund program must be conducted first with the major emphasis on giving. In no sense should this program be moderated or cut back because a bond program is planned. Utilize the capital-fund program to the highest degree. Then, allow a reasonable period of time before scheduling the bond program. Ideally, the two programs should be separated by about a year. This will allow time for other church program emphases and will eliminate potential pressure if the bond program immediately follows the capital-fund effort.

Finance committees should be cautious of notes or bond issues with balloon provisions. These are arrangements which allow lower payments for several years and then assess a large payment that, in effect, compensates for the lower payments. The arrangement is based on the theory that the growth of the church will provide more than adequate finances to cover the balloon note when it comes due. That is always a risky assumption. Sound financial plans are based on present resources, not future growth possibilities.

A church should limit its long-term indebtedness to fifteen years. In fact, most churches should amortize loans within ten years. In a few instances, churches may have to stretch payments to twenty years. Dragging them out for twenty-five years is a mistake because there is only a minimal difference in monthly payments between a twenty and a twenty-five-year loan ($48 less per $100,000 at 12 percent). However, four of the five years gained in a twenty-five-year loan are required just to pay the additional interest between a twenty and twenty-five-year term. A twenty-year loan reduces monthly payments by only $99 per $100,000 under a fifteen-year term at 12 percent interest. Three and one-half of the extra five years gained are required just to pay the additional interest. Study the chart in figure 10 for other comparisons.

Comparison of Long-Term Loans
(Per $100,000 at 12 Percent Interest)

	Monthly Payments Reduced	Additional Interest Paid
From 15 to 20 Years	$99	$48,300
From 15 to 25 Years	$147	$100,020
From 20 to 25 Years	$48	$51,720

FIGURE 10

Monthly Payments Per $1,000 Necessary to Amortize a Loan

Term	10%	11%	12%	13%	14%
7 Years	$16.61	$17.13	$17.66	$18.20	$18.75
10 Years	13.22	13.78	14.35	14.94	15.53
15 Years	10.75	11.37	12.01	12.66	13.32
20 Years	9.66	10.33	11.02	11.72	12.44

FIGURE 11

Notes

1. Carl Hoffman, "Four Times in a Row," *The Baptist Program*, January 1991, 12.

6

Selecting and Working with the Architect

by Steven Newton, A.I.A.

Buildings built to the glory of God have stretched the abilities and imaginations of the faithful from the time of Solomon until the present. In increasing measure, building for today's church is a complex process requiring a combination of expertise, knowledge, and skill. These valuable and essential tools are available to the church through specially qualified professionals. While the building industry provides the materials and services needed for the actual construction of the facility, the architect works with the church to develop an appropriate design response to the church's program requirements. During construction the architect acts as the church's agent in working with the building industry to achieve that design in the completed facility.

Even with the legal requirements and complexities involved, questions such as the following are often asked:

"Why do we need to go to the expense of hiring an architect?"

"All we really need is a building, so why not just go out and get a contractor to build it for us?"

"Isn't an architect just going to run up the cost?"

These questions reflect a widespread misunderstanding of the architect's role. Actually, the cost of the architect should be viewed as an investment, not as an unnecessary expense.

The church entering a building program is preparing to invest an enormous amount of God's resources. In the parable of the talents (Matt. 25:14-30), which servant did the master commend and reward? Not the one who had spent the least money but the one who most wisely invested the resources he was given. The right architect working with a focused, diligent committee will propose an excellent investment of resources that will benefit the church far beyond the initial expense.

Selecting the Architect

How does one find the "right" architect? An architect's license or listing in the phone book does not automatically qualify him or her to design the building most suitable for the needs of the church. The selection of the architect is vitally important to the success of the building project. The architect will play a significant role in the allocation of the church's resources for the construction project. Therefore, the utmost care and attention should be given to the selection process.

The best approach to architectural selection is a well-planned, carefully conducted interview process. To begin this process, prepare a list of potential candidates. The candidates can be found through referrals from other churches, church members, or other trustworthy sources. Also consider architects who have contacted the church or denominational offices to express interest in providing services. The church that is considering future construction would be wise to keep a file of contacts in anticipation of this need.

If the list of architects is fairly extensive, initial efforts should reduce it to no more than five or six. Contact the candidates by letter with an invitation to submit written information about the firm and a statement of qualifications for services related to the specific project under consideration. Provide a description of the professional services desired as well as the anticipated scope of construction. If possible, provide the opportunity for the architect to meet with key committee or church leaders and provide access to the potential site and any existing buildings. Equal access should be available to all candidates. Evaluate the architects' responses to determine which candidates to interview. This evaluation is usually performed by a designated subcommittee. The number of architects interviewed should not exceed five. This is beneficial in two ways: (1) it helps keep the interviewers fresh; and (2) it communicates to the architect the serious interest and intent of the church. Both contribute to a quality interview.

The primary criteria for interviewing should focus on professional reputation and competence as these relate to the proposed project. This may be difficult if material sent by several firms appears to be similar. The architect's statement of qualifications should include a list of similar or related projects with references. The committee must be sure to contact references for each candidate. They should ask why that architect was chosen, if his performance met expectations, and if they would choose to work with him again. They must not be afraid to ask probing questions, especially if the reference appears to hesitate in a response. This information will help make a more informed distinction between candidates. If the committee believes that a firm would not be right for the church's project, they should probably choose not to interview that firm.

Size of the firm is not necessarily a good criteria in judging design capabilities. Small firms make up a significant majority of architectural firms in the United States, and many are capable of a broad range of services, including the design of large, complex buildings. Even in larger firms, the number of people who actually work on a given project is surprisingly small. More important are the capabilities of the personnel who will actually be involved in the church's project. These persons should be given careful consideration throughout the interview process.

An exhaustive list of church project involvement in the past does not automatically qualify one architect over the other. The intent of the prequalification phase is to create a manageable group of qualified candidates for an unbiased interview, not to narrow the list down to one.

The actual interview can be an enjoyable, educational time for the committee as well as the candidate. The church committee should work to create an open, professional environment in which communication and exchange of thoughts and ideas can take place. The committee should remember that the architect has a lot to offer to the church and will be evaluating the church during the interview process as well. The committee which seeks to intimidate or establish an adversarial atmosphere at the interview will miss an opportunity to effectively evaluate the most important criterion for selection: the ability of the candidate to understand and accomplish the building goals of the church.

A thorough understanding of the church and its goals can come only as a result of an open, honest relationship between the church and the architect. During the interview, the committee must be prepared to evaluate such intangibles as compatibility and commitment to the church's goals. This will involve many of the same dynamics required for all interpersonal relationships.

One key interview factor is time. An effective interview will not take place in thirty minutes. Adequate time must be allowed, usually sixty to ninety minutes. Interviews should not be crowded together. One interview per session, or at most two, will help keep the committee fresh and will avoid information overload. If two interviews are scheduled during a session, allow fifteen to thirty minutes between interviews for time overruns and breaks.

Before making a final selection or decision, the committee may wish to bring one or more candidates back for a follow-up interview. In this follow-up, more specifics can be dealt with as they relate to the project at hand. Perhaps after or during the previous interview, some questions were raised which need clarification. The follow-up can be a time to get to know the candidate better. This time can help prepare for the possible relationship to follow.

Consider the relatively small church in a rural community which interviewed several architects and then brought their top candidate back for two more interviews before making a final selection. Some would say the committee was too meticulous, but when they made their decision, they had their questions answered and felt unanimously they had made the right choice. They felt good about the professionals they would be dealing with for the next two years and were confident their goals and concerns were understood. The completed project resulted in a greatly enhanced facility for ministry which bears witness to the care and diligence of the committee in the selection of the architect.

A list of sample interview questions is included in appendix D. The basic selection criteria can be summarized in the following categories:

- Capability to perform the project under consideration
- Compatibility in working with the committee

- Commitment to achieving the goals of the church
- Cost control in professional fees and overall project budget

The most successful selection will be made when a proper balance of all the above criteria is sought. The first three have been mentioned in preceding paragraphs. The latter category, cost control, often gets the most attention but is probably the least understood.

The church which does not place a priority on cost control is rare indeed. In fact, wise stewardship principles demand that the church seek the best possible investment of its financial resources. This does not, however, suggest that the committee should place emphasis on the lowest fee as a criterion for selection of the architect. Comparison of fees is appropriate and should be given attention. However, design fees are a relatively small percentage of the total project budget and should not be the sole basis for selecting an architect. (See ch. 5 for a discussion of the project budget.)

More important than the fee is the ability of the architect to achieve the goals of the church while working within established budget parameters. By designing site and buildings the architect is placed in a position of managing vast amounts of the church's financial resources. Construction costs will often run two to three times a church's annual budget. Seemingly minor decisions can have significant impact on construction cost, and these decisions are influenced by the architect throughout the course of a project. With this in mind, the committee should recognize that the lowest fee does not necessarily represent the greatest investment value.

Contracting with the Architect

The best church building projects result when responsible church representatives and architects form good professional and often personal relationships. These relationships are formed early in the planning process. They are nourished by clear communication, mutually understood expectations, and a willingness of both client and professional to understand their responsibilities for realizing a successful project. Once the architect is selected and general expectations discussed, a formal agreement should be negotiated. The agreement between the church and the architect assures that both parties understand the project and agree on requirements and expectations. The following are areas which need to be addressed prior to finalizing the agreement:

- Project scope—what is to be designed and built?
- Project site—where will (might) it be built?
- Levels of quality in amenities, finishes, and architectural detail
- Special equipment or requirements (music, sound, kitchen, etc.)
- Budget estimate and sources of financing
- Tentative progress schedule including design reviews and target date for completion
- Key representatives to whom the architect will be responsible
- Architect's fee structure

Experienced committees recognize that adequate compensation for the architect is in their best interest, for it helps to assure the type and level of service needed to fulfill their expectations. Even so, there are a number of acceptable ways to structure design fees:

1. *The stipulated sum or "fixed fee" is generally preferred.*—This fee arrangement requires that the proposed project be fairly well defined in scope. It will allow the church to more accurately budget design fees as a part of the total project budget.
2. *A fee based on a percentage of construction cost is often negotiated.*—This allows flexibility when the project scope has not been fully defined. The design fee varies with the scope of the work.
3. *Compensation at an hourly rate is generally used for a small project or one with a number of unknown variables.*—It can sometimes be employed to explore design options prior to committing to an architect for the full scope of architectural services.

No matter which option is taken, the agreement should be formalized in a contract. Even though goodwill is intended by both parties, no handshake is firm enough to reach all the understandings about the roles and obligations of the owner and the architect. One of the AIA Owner-Architect agreements is usually desirable. These standard forms of agreement, first developed by the American Institute of Architects in the 1880s, have been carefully reviewed and modified over the years. They are widely used and present a consensus among organizations representing owners, lawyers, contractors, engineers, and architects. They are "coordinated" to fit together with other AIA agreements, which will be important when establishing the construction contract (see ch. 9).

Distinction should be made between the architect's basic services and other indirect costs which the church may incur. Under most AIA Owner-Architect Agreements the basic services are listed under five major project phases:

- Schematic Design Phase
- Design Development Phase
- Construction Documents Phase
- Bidding or Negotiating Phase
- Construction Contract Administration Phase

The basic services relative to these phases include all services required to design the basic building and surrounding site. This includes structural, mechanical, plumbing, electrical, and, usually, civil design. These all come under the umbrella of architectural services. Unless specified in advance as part of the formal agreement, the basic services do not include interior design services, landscape design services, acoustical design, specialized equipment layout, or predesign services such as existing facilities surveys, detailed site utilization studies, environmental studies, or zoning processing. These services ordinarily fall under the heading of additional services as outlined in the AIA agreements. The church and the architect should have a clear understanding about which are basic services and which are additional services. Through mutual agreement, services can be customized under the AIA agreements.

The architect's fees generally cover only the professional services provided and do not cover expenses for travel, mileage, long-distance phone calls, photocopying, reproduction of project-related documents, renderings, and models. The committee should clarify each of these items with the architect and make necessary adjustments at the beginning. The committee may wish to include renderings or models as a basic service or obtain a firm cost for these as an additional service. The other items are negotiable.

Working with the Architect

Establish an orderly process for planning and designing the church facility. Once a clear statement of project requirements is established and all contractual arrangements made with the architect, the project can proceed through the designated phases, outlined in the AIA agreements.

Schematic Design Phase

This phase involves a preliminary evaluation of the project budget and the statement of building requirements prepared by the church. Project scope, quality, and cost combine to create a critical balance in every construction project. The first two of these variables can be controlled in design; the current market determines cost. The church will need to establish priorities among these variables and set acceptable ranges for each. Then, the architect can provide alternative approaches to the design and construction of the project. Based on the preferred design approach, the mutually agreed upon project requirements, and the budget, the architect can prepare drawings and other documentation illustrating the preliminary design. This should be accompanied by a statement of probable construction cost and should be thoroughly reviewed by the committee.

Design Development Phase

Based on approval of the schematic design documents, the architect can proceed to prepare more detailed design development documents which thoroughly describe the scope, size, and character of the construction project. This includes information related to structural, mechanical, and electrical systems; materials; and other architectural elements necessary to provide a more detailed construction cost statement.

Construction Documents Phase

Following approval of the design development documents, the architect will prepare construction documents consisting of drawings and specifications setting forth in detail the construction requirements of the project. The drawings primarily describe location and quantity of building components while the specifications relate to quality and execution of the construction work. Omitting either of these portions of the construction documents could leave the church open to unpleasant surprises as work progresses. As a part of the services related to this phase, the architect should assist the church in the preparation of materials necessary for bidding or negotiating the construction contract and for necessary government approvals.

Bidding or Negotiation Phase

During this phase the architect will assist the church in obtaining bids or negotiated proposals from contractors and then

MODELS AND RENDERINGS ARE EFFECTIVE IN COMMUNICATING A DESIGN CONCEPT.

assist in preparing the contracts for construction. While this phase usually occurs in sequence after the construction documents phase, in a negotiated construction contract arrangement the architect and committee involve the contractor at an earlier stage (see ch. 9). With this arrangement, the services related to this phase would overlap with previous phases.

The architect and committee should consider the possibility of establishing several alternates for the bidding process. An alternate identifies a specific part of the construction project which may be eliminated at the discretion of the committee. The alternate must be clearly defined in the construction documents. Obviously, the alternate must be a part of the construction that is not essential to the overall integrity of the project. Provisions can be made to add the alternate at a later date. For example, the bidding instructions might request a base bid on the total project and three alternates:

1. Alternate one might deduct the cost of constructing the music rehearsal wing.
2. Alternate two might deduct the cost of movable walls in the fellowship hall.
3. Alternate three might deduct the cost of developing and paving an expansion to the parking area.

Notice that each of these are deduct alternates. Usually, deduct alternates will produce more competitive bids than add alternates because the latter may not be viewed by the contractor as a high-priority item. Another possibility is that a contractor is not really interested in bidding on the add alternate but will submit a high bid just to fulfill the request.

The purpose of establishing the alternate process is to control the final cost. By making this a part of the bidding process a church can obtain competitive estimates for each of the alternates. The church that simply obtains a base bid and then negotiates with the low bidder for alternates is losing the advantage of competitive bidding. Once a contractor knows he is the low bidder, his alternate bids may not be developed as competitively as they would be in the initial process.

Construction Administration Phase

The architect, acting as the church's representative during the building phase, interprets the construction documents. He works to guard the church against defects and deficiencies in the construction. This task is important, but many committees misunderstand the actual responsibilities. The architect does not supervise construction or have responsibility for construction means, techniques, sequences, or procedures. This responsibility belongs to the contractor. The architect does visit the site at appropriate intervals, evaluates the progress of the work, and renders impartial interpretations of the contract documents. He has the authority under AIA documents to reject work not conforming with the contract documents.

Additionally, the architect authorizes payment requests by the contractor, if they reflect the amount of work actually performed. This helps protect the church from financial loss in case of the contractor's default on the project. Most of the time the lending institution for the project requires this certification for their own protection. Some states and municipalities require that this service be performed and certified by the architect prior to allowing building occupancy.

Alternate Design Arrangements

A word of caution should be expressed concerning alternate design arrangements or the employment of paraprofessionals for building design. The relationship between church and architect obviously requires a significant investment of time and professional expertise. Any arrangement which reduces the time and development of the relationship, or which introduces a third party intermediary between the church and designer, inevitably affects the finished product.

The goal to construct the most effective facility for mission and ministry should not be compromised. Most people in need of serious medical attention would avoid the surgeon who proposed to make a diagnosis without proper firsthand contact with the patient or who proposed to perform surgery through a less qualified third party. In the same way, the church that is serious about its investment of resources and mission purpose will insist upon a qualified professional who will guard the church's interests to the greatest possible extent. Most alternate design arrangements offer a minor reduction in costs and a major reduction in professional service.

Architecture is by nature a labor-intensive profession which functions in a highly competitive marketplace. Variation between fees is minimal for the most part and any significant deviation probably reflects a corresponding variation in service. This is not a suggestion to not seek the best value but merely to point out the need for extreme care in a decision of such long-term implications.

Teamwork Brings the Best Results

The church receives the greatest value for its investment when all parties diligently work toward a common goal—the mission of the church. The building-steering committee must work hard throughout the course of the project to create a spirit of teamwork with the architect, contractor, and other related parties.

Communication is essential for the effective fulfillment of the church's goals and expectations. The committee should take a leadership role in establishing clear channels of communication. Decisiveness is required to keep the project running smoothly. The church should insist upon all information needed to make an informed decision and then proceed with a clear, timely response. All decisions and all appropriate communication by the architect, the church, or the contractor should be recorded in writing. Minutes of each meeting should be recorded and distributed to each party involved.

Some decisions may not be pleasant, and there may be strained relationships at times. A strong commitment to teamwork on the part of all parties will help smooth the rough spots so the team can move on with the important work at hand.

If this sounds like a lot of responsibility for the architect and the church, it is. Each person related to the process of design and construction will have significant individual roles as well as shared responsibilities for the success of the project. The best and most rewarding results will occur when all parties work together in a spirit of teamwork and cooperation with a shared commitment to the best interests of the church.

7

Utilizing Wise Space Design Principles

by Steven Newton, A.I.A.

The properly designed church facility is distinctive. Just as the body of Christ is exhorted to be in the world but not of it, to be salt and light in the world, so the church building should suggest in some way the nature of God and His people. Building themes can be drawn from the attributes of God as revealed through Scripture and the Holy Spirit, such as power, strength, compassion, love, and holiness. Though we have excellent examples to compare and admire, there is no set formula that defines what a church building must look like. It can take on the appearance of a school, but not just a school; a house, but not just any house; an assembly hall, but not an assembly hall only. Paradoxically, while projecting distinctiveness, it should relate to the surrounding community just as Christ related personally with those of His community and ministry.

The well-designed church facility will offer an optimum balance between these three critical variables: project scope, quality, and cost. As a three-legged stool with unequal legs becomes virtually useless for its intended purpose, the church facility which reflects a disregard for design balance in these three areas is limited in its ability to accommodate the mission of the church. The architect is a valuable resource person but should not be expected to make a complete and accurate assessment of this balance without significant communication, evaluation, and dialogue with the building-steering committee. This is part of the purpose of the project phases and progress reviews. In these reviews, the committee and the architect move through the process together. A thorough understanding of the design presented by the architect is necessary for meaningful evaluation. The

CHURCH BUILDINGS VARY GREATLY IN DESIGN.

architect should present the design in layman's terms in the clearest possible manner, taking whatever time is needed to answer questions and make clarifications to the satisfaction of all committee members. Graphic illustrations will assist in these presentations. Ideally, the architect, the steering committee, and, at some point, the contractor work together to achieve optimum design balance.

The committee will need to know what to look for in evaluating the design presented by the architect. The following represent key characteristics of a well-designed church facility.

Functional

The church facility should be designed to support the mission of the church. The design must address the program requirements developed by the building-steering committee. No matter what shape the building takes, space should be arranged in an orderly manner with ample and clearly defined circulation areas. Site access and parking are important design considerations. Conveniently located and easily visible entrances will be an asset to church members and assist newcomers in finding their way. Gathering space at the entrance to assembly areas will avoid congestion and encourage fellowship in the congregation.

Flexible

While some spaces in the church facility will be designed for specific functions, other spaces should be designed for the greatest possible flexibility in usage. Space which is too rigidly designed can become an obstacle to the church's mission and growth. In some instances, design flexibility takes the form of multiuse space which allows for more frequent and varied use of the facility. While multiple use is not the answer in every situation, it allows the church to accommodate greater capacity and extended ministries. Care must be exercised in multiuse space not to shortchange the quality of the primary function.

Flexibility also allows for future program changes or building expansion. These possibilities should be considered and provision made for them in the initial construction. This is particularly

WELL-DESIGNED ENTRANCES, GATHERING AREAS, AND CIRCULATION SPACE ARE COMPONENTS OF A "USER-FRIENDLY" BUILDING.

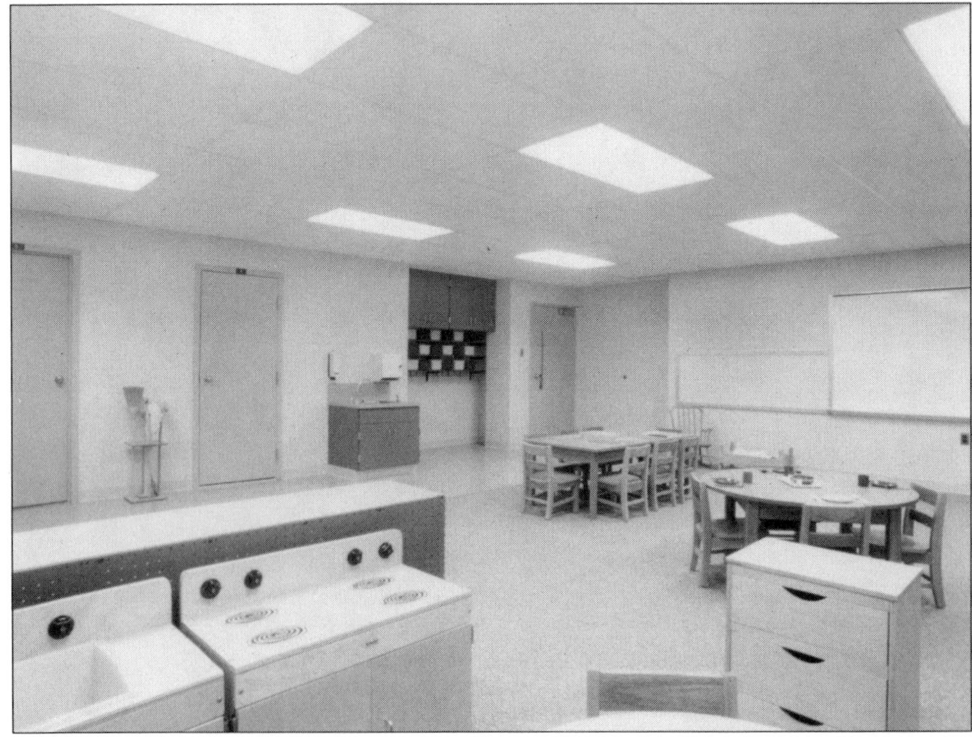

true when structural considerations are involved. For example, allowances for future elevators, stairwells, connectors, balconies, or additional floors can be readily accommodated through proper planning and comparatively little expense. Adding them to an existing building where no provisions have been made can be extremely expensive or even cost prohibitive. For similar reasons, avoid load-bearing interior walls.

Attractive

Looking at creation, we know that God is not indifferent to beauty and order. The well-designed church building should project beauty and order in its appearance, both interior and exterior. It will make a positive statement about the church's values. In fact, the church building design in many cases offers an important first impression to many people not already associated with the church.

Exterior Design

Product retailers put much emphasis on packaging and visual advertising because visual images make strong and lasting impressions. The church must consider the impression it wishes to make in its community through the exterior design of the building. Like a billboard, it will be seen by passing motorists who may have no other contact with the church. It will make an impression on the newcomer to the community or the one who is seeking a church home. It will offer a testimony about the church's values, often long before someone meets church members.

Therefore, the church must be careful what it says through building design. Will the building suggest permanence, strength, refuge, warmth, welcome, austerity, vitality, or possibly a combination of some of these and other characteristics? Will the building design relate positively to the surrounding environment? Will the building design withstand the test of time, reflecting a timeless design quality, or will it reflect a dated architectural style? Will the design evoke emotions of joy and praise to God? These are questions the church must answer.

This should in no way imply that extravagance is necessary or

Various Designs For Flexible Space In Church Buildings.

Strong Visible Images Make Lasting Impressions.

An Addition To A Church Facility Should Relate To Existing Structures.

even desirable. More important than the cost of the materials is the way they are utilized and blended; the form, shape, and proportion which they take; and the way they relate to the surrounding environment. This can be effectively accomplished in all ranges of cost. On the other hand, expensive construction does not guarantee good design. While good design is usually apparent to the layperson once it is experienced, it is difficult for most people to define. These matters fall under the expertise of the professional and underscore the importance of selecting the right architect as outlined in chapter 6.

Interior Design

The exterior design should be translated in some way into the interior of the building. This is often accomplished in terms of material, color, texture, style, and volume of space. For instance, a building with traditional styling will continue that pattern in the interior details. A vaulted ceiling in a worship center can be visible in the exterior building form. At times, the exterior material will be brought into interior spaces to make a visual and textural connection. Window patterns and skylights seen from the outside can strengthen this important relationship. By relating the interior to the exterior the building expresses consistent design. This creates a comfortable transition as a person experiences the building first at a distance, then at close range, then inside.

Volume of space should be appropriate to the intended use. In a large or congested space a higher ceiling helps avoid a compressed or confined feeling. Well-coordinated window treatment and interior details provide a sense of rhythm and proportion of space.

Color and lighting are key components of well-designed interior space. Color influences people, causing them to feel warm or cool, happy or depressed. A sense of feeling welcome, worshipful, or receptive to instruction will all be influenced by color. Proper use of color can bring space to life, while a poorly coordinated color scheme can detract from the effectiveness of the space.

Lighting can be utilized to create an appropriate environment for various functions: worship, teaching, meditation, fellowship activities, and special focus or displays. Lighting techniques can make a space seem wider or taller and can encourage a spirit of serenity or joy. With lighting, remember, more is not always better. Indirect lighting can be an especially effective tool. Natural lighting is generally encouraged, but control must be considered for daytime use of multimedia. Lighting behind a speaker should be indirect or subdued to avoid silhouetting or glare.

Safe

The church has a responsibility to provide for the safety of those who enter its buildings. Building codes provide a guide as well as legal requirements for the protection of public safety. They have become increasingly stringent in recent years as regulatory agencies have increased their enforcement of the adopted codes. Every church facility in the United States falls

EXTERIOR LIGHTING IS IMPORTANT FOR VISIBILITY AND SECURITY.

under building codes. Some locales are not as persistent in enforcement as others. The church should go the extra mile in meeting code requirements to ensure safety and to set a positive example in the community.

Almost all locally adopted building codes follow one of the three models: National Building Code, Standard Building Code, or Uniform Building Code.

Even codes which have been modified for local conditions and adopted as city, county, or state codes generally reflect a major influence of and similar format to one of these codes. In addition to these codes, a fourth encompasses the entire country and is published by the National Fire Protection Association: the Life Safety Code. All of these codes contain requirements which have a great impact on church building design. Multiuse facilities for church schools or day-care activities are subject to additional requirements.

Code requirements must be addressed in the design process. Once the building is under construction, the correction of code violations can be extremely expensive or totally unfeasible. One church built a worship facility with the intention of finishing a balcony area as soon as funds were available. Even though the balcony platform was in place, the access stairs were inadequate for the occupant load, and the church was unable to complete the structure. Another church started construction with the understanding that no permit was required by the county. A state inspector driving by noticed the construction and proceeded to stop work on the project until state requirements could be met. This required changing the building design. These circumstances can be avoided through careful code analysis during the design and construction documents phases.

Building codes change constantly, making it difficult for even the professional to address every issue. It is a good idea to review preliminary building designs with code officials. This allows early discussion of concepts and plans relative to life safety and code concerns. Usually, this is beneficial to the code officials as well as the church, as it familiarizes them with the project. Areas of concern can be addressed early in the process. In this way, everyone can work together toward the common goal: the safety of the building occupants. The architect should take a leadership role in these discussions so that all requirements can be properly incorporated into the building design.

Handicapped Accessible

Provision for the physically handicapped is required in all new construction and in renovation of existing facilities. Federal, state, and local codes have established minimum standards for such provisions. Churches should take the lead in meeting these codes, but sometimes they fail to do so. While there are many kinds of physical handicaps, the codes focus on wheelchair access. Although there are many specific requirements, most handicapped accommodation requirements reflect common sense. See chapter 9 for discussion and illustrations of code requirements.

Elements intended to aid in handicapped access should be integrated into the building design as discreetly as possible. Often, accessibility requirements can be incorporated in such a way as to be useful to all building occupants. This also benefits handicapped persons because they prefer integration into the congregation.

Economical

Economy in building design can be achieved in a number of forms, but these do not necessarily represent lowest initial construction cost. True economy occurs when the church maximizes stewardship of its resources. True economy is measured in terms of building **value** rather than building cost.

Economy is achieved when the church judiciously establishes a realistic, affordable project budget, and then carefully maintains that budget through the course of the project. Adequate budgeting will allow the committee to make decisions relative to long-term rather than initial costs. Cutting corners on the front end can often lead to greater long-term costs. The result is usually evident in the building design. Good design reflects a consistency of cost control throughout with appropriate attention given to long-term building value.

The church should be especially skeptical of very low construction cost projections. Sometimes low projections are made to gain advantage, sometimes they reflect what the committee wants to hear, and sometimes there is an honest but mistaken belief in the accuracy of such projections. Whatever the cause, low-cost projections can led a committee to make unwise decisions relative to the allocation of funds. Often, this error is not discovered until construction is well underway, resulting in excessive borrowing or even inability to finish the project because of lack of funds.

Maintenance and energy efficiency are certainly factors in building economy. Coordinating material selection and technical detailing creates a well-designed facility that operates as trouble-free as possible. Roofs should be planned and constructed to allow for drainage as quickly as possible. Church buildings are not particularly good applications for flat-roof structures unless the church has an adequate maintenance program and staff. Use interior and exterior materials which will stand up to wear and which require a minimum of maintenance. Energy efficiency creates obvious long-term savings and does not necessarily require excessive initial cost (see ch. 8).

Professional Assistance

The primary source of professional assistance for the church during the course of a construction project is the local architect. He will be able to give consistent, on-site attention to the needs of the church and should have the expertise required to adequately assist the church in reaching its building objective.

8

Building for Operational Efficiency

Initial concerns about building costs focus on construction. Few committees give serious attention in their early planning to projected operational costs. That can be a serious mistake, for the latter costs occur as long as the building is used. Therefore, selecting design, materials, and finishes with no regard for long-term costs can be extremely expensive. Cutting $50,000 in construction costs is a bad bargain if it increases annual operational costs by $10,000. That would amount to paying 20 percent on the money saved every year the building is used—an expensive financial miscue. Therefore, a wise committee will give serious attention to life-cycle cost analysis, energy conservation measures, full utilization of space, and maintenance estimates.

Operational costs are determined by programing, scheduling, and provisions for energy efficiency. The optimum results can be obtained only when each of these three factors is handled responsibly. To focus on either and neglect the others can lead to excessive operational costs.

Space Utilization and Scheduling

One way to ensure efficient operational costs is to make the best use of flexible space, including the possibility of scheduling multiple services or multiple Sunday Schools.

Space Utilization

One of the first issues to consider is the potential savings obtained with multiuse and multipurpose space. Churches utilizing these space concepts can reduce by as much as 20 percent the total amount of space required for a single-use space design.

That can cut the cost of construction by 15 to 20 percent. It can also significantly reduce maintenance and operational costs. Once the space is conditioned for a service or activity, the cost of using it immediately thereafter for another service is significantly less than the cost of conditioning it for first-time use. Consider also that maintenance costs for double-use space are little more than for single-use space. Therefore, the per person cost of double-use space is only about half the cost of single-use space.

Scheduling

Scheduling considerations should also be evaluated as a part of planning for operational efficiency. Churches conducting dual services can accommodate up to 85 to 90 percent more people in the same amount of space. Some leaders think in terms of increasing the capacity by 100 percent with dual services. However, that is not practical for two reasons: (1) younger preschoolers are in the same space for the full period on Sunday morning, so this space cannot be used twice, and (2) securing an equal number in attendance in each service is next to impossible.

Think of the significant savings that could be achieved by scheduling dual services. Consider the fact that much of an average church building is used less than three hours per week. Does that represent the best stewardship of resources? Why not explore the possibility of scheduling dual services in the same space?

The arguments against dual services are often presented in a convincing manner.

- Dual services tend to divide a church into two different congregations.
- Dual services will not have the same impact because all the congregation is not together at the same time.
- Preaching twice on Sunday morning creates an unreasonable workload for the pastor.
- Sufficient, trained leadership to conduct dual services is not available in our church.
- Our people will just not accept the changed schedules required by dual services.
- We tried dual services once and our people did not like them; so we returned to our old schedule.

There is no question but that dual services meet with mixed response from different congregations. Some churches find immediate acceptance and glowing success with dual services. In fact, many churches find such a high degree of acceptance with these services they never expect to change back to single services. They have found their people appreciate the flexibility of scheduling that gives them alternative times for worship and Bible study. Leaders believe they reach more people because of this flexibility. They feel fellowship is enhanced and the personal touch is easier to maintain with dual services. After all, how many people can one personally "touch" and converse with before or after church services? There is, of course, value in seeing friends even if there is no opportunity for personal exchange, but there surely is a limit to the number one can even "see" in any kind of meaningful manner.

Other churches try dual services and immediately find resistance and objections to the schedule. Some of this may come from a predisposition to oppose what is new and different. However, in many instances the negative reaction may come in a more subtle way. It may come because the leadership has not adequately prepared the church for the new schedule. The congregation as a whole may not feel they were consulted before the decision was made. They may not understand why the change is being proposed. Adequate information about the alternatives to dual services may not have been communicated. Perhaps the greatest resistance comes because fears relative to dual services have not been openly discussed and answered. There may be no strategy in place for dealing with the sense of separation that can come with dual services. If dual services are initiated in a tenuous or doubting climate, they will not have a good chance of acceptance. Therefore, no one should be surprised when the congregation's worst fears are realized.

All the negative arguments about dual services do not answer the questions about wise stewardship of space that is used less than three hours a week. Granted, dual services may call for some adjustments and even some inconveniences, but is it not possible that our Lord expects that response from us? Is it not possible that He expects us to bring creativity and innovation to these issues? The pressing needs for mission support, ministry resources, and personnel call church leaders to serious and prayerful evaluation of all plans for new buildings.

This is especially true when the plans involve high interest payments that could be avoided by scheduling dual services for several years. For instance, a large church must either go to dual services or build new space. The building will cost $500,000 and the church has no funds on hand. They can build immediately and finance construction costs for fifteen years, or they can go to dual services for three years while they are raising funds for building. If they choose the first option and build immediately, they will pay about $470,000 in interest in addition to the $500,000. If they choose the second option and build three years later, they will pay only $8,000 in interest. The difference in interest is about $12,800 per month for the three-year period. How many members would be opposed to dual services for three years at a monthly savings of $12,800?

Energy-Efficient Buildings

Planning for operational efficiency must also include consideration of energy costs. These can be controlled somewhat through proper design, efficient systems and equipment, and adequate study.

Energy-Efficient Design

Orientation of building on site.—The starting point for energy-efficient design is orientation of the building on the property. If possible, the building should be situated so that main entrances are not on the north side. Remember, the north side of the building may not get direct sun in the winter. In some climates, ice and snow can build up in this area and create hazardous conditions. Prevailing winter winds from the north also can add to infiltration problems at main entrances. The building should be oriented to effectively utilize passive solar. This involves a plan that will admit the direct rays of the sun in the winter and block them in the summer. Fins and overhangs can be used for this purpose if the building is properly oriented on the site. (See fig. 12 for an illustration.)

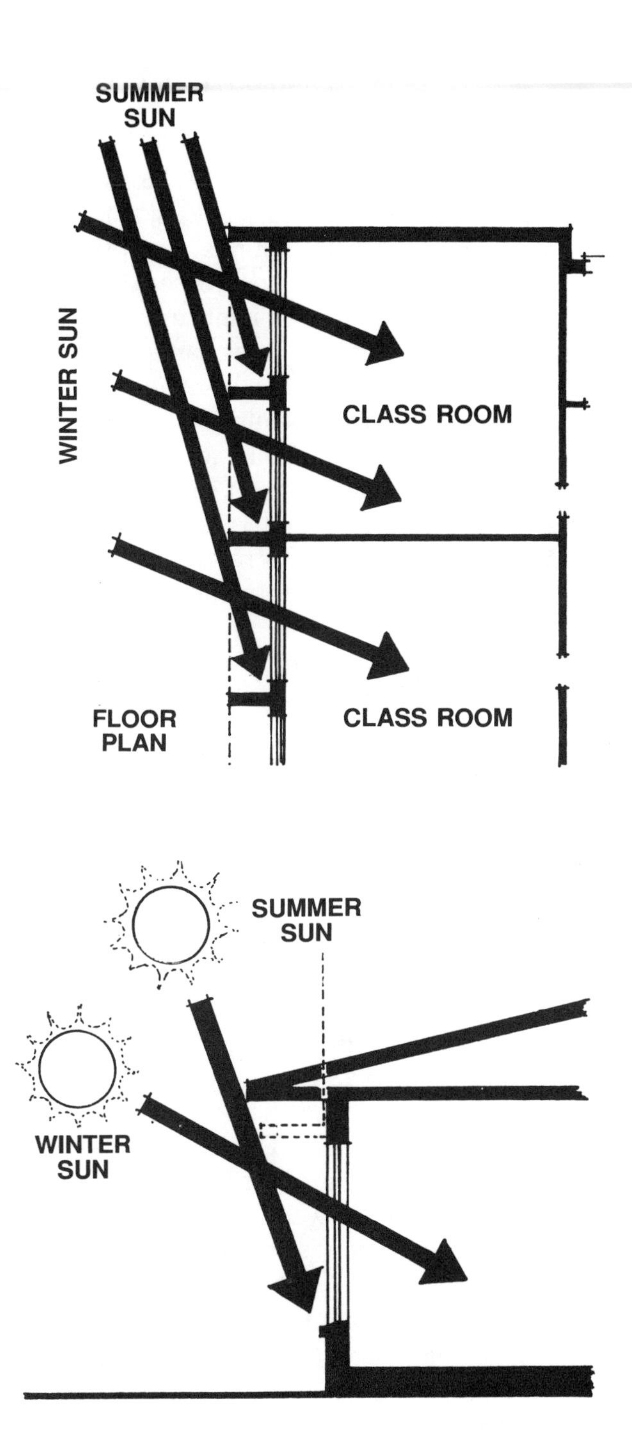

FIGURE 12: FINS AND OVERHANGS SHIELD WINDOWS

Landscaping for energy conservation.—A landscape plan that is sensitive to energy conservation can make significant contributions to the project. Berms (earth mounds) and plantings can be designed to serve as windbreaks to decrease wind velocity and thereby reduce heat loss of the building envelope and shield entrances (see fig. 13). Deciduous trees can shade the building in the summer and then allow the sun to help warm it in the winter (see fig. 14). Well-placed plantings can help prevent the reflection of summer heat into the building.

Air locks at main entrances.—A major cause of heat loss in the winter and heat gain in the summer is the opening of exterior doors. Infiltration at entrances can be reduced by as much as 85 percent by adding air locks or double entry at major entrances (see fig. 15).

Double glazing and insulating glass.—Exterior glass loses about ten times as much heat as an insulated masonry wall. Therefore, all exterior glass areas should have thermopane or double glazing, and/or insulated glass. Thermopane or double glazing can reduce heat loss by as much as 50 percent. Insulating glass is available with varying performance ratings. Manufacturers of low-emissivity coated glass claim as much as a 70 percent reduction in heat loss with their product. The low-E coatings are designed to reflect heat back into the heated space. Controlling the amount and location of exterior glass can also reduce energy consumption. In the winter, generally, north-facing glassed areas will lose heat whereas south-facing glassed areas save heat because of passive solar gain.

Insulation.—One of the basic factors affecting heat loss and heat gain in a building is transfer. This is the process by which heat is transferred through the exterior of the building envelope. The envelope includes exterior walls, windows, doors, roof, and floor. The rate of transfer depends on the various components of the building envelope and the difference between outside and inside temperatures. A basic principle is that heat is always conducted from an area of higher temperature to an area of lower temperature. In the summer, heat is transferred through the envelope into an air-conditioned building. In the winter, indoor heat is transferred through the envelope to the exterior.

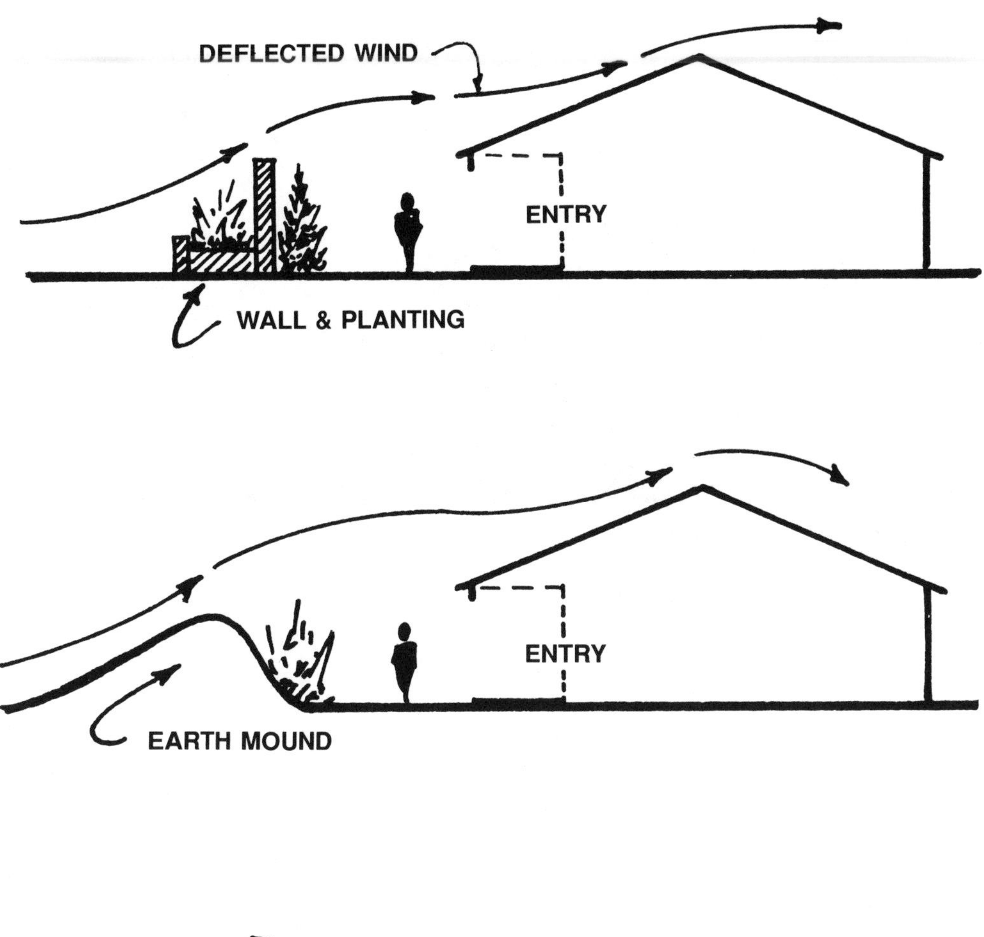

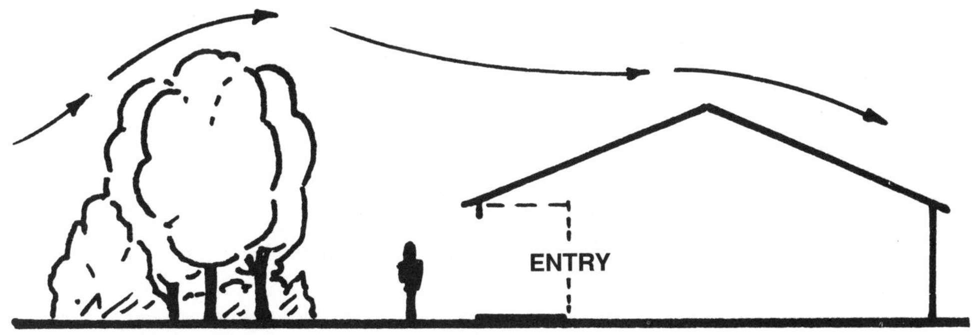

FIGURE 13: PLANTINGS AND EARTH MOUNDS SHIELD ENTRANCES

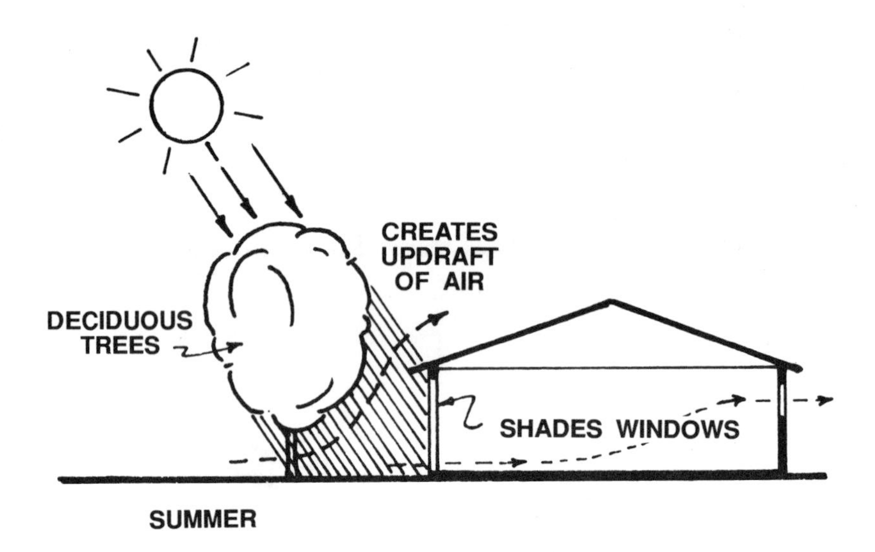

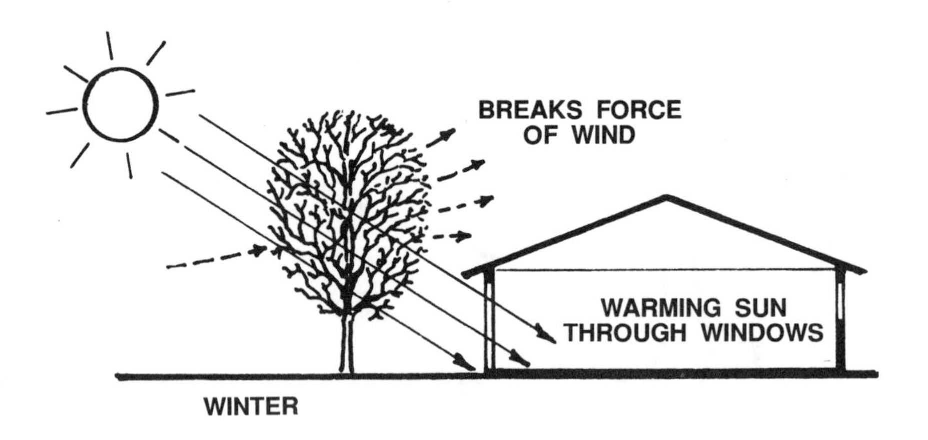

FIGURE 14: DECIDUOUS TREES SHIELD YEAR-ROUND

One of the goals of wise design is to use materials that reduce the rate of transfer.

Insulation is designed to accomplish this in various ways, including reflection, impeding air flow, and slowing the process of conduction. A dead-air space is a good insulator, but moving air facilitates heat flow. The primary reason double glazing is so effective is not the additional sheet of glass but the dead-air space between the two sheets of glass. Materials used for insulation include fiberglass, cellulose fiber, and various foam products such as Styrofoam and polystyrene. These are rated according to their thermal resistance (R-value). The higher the R-value the more resistance there is to heat flow. A dramatic indication of the effectiveness of insulation can be seen from the following equation. Six inches of fiberglass batts are approximately equal to the R-value of fifteen inches of solid wood which is approximately equal to the R-value of a solid common brick wall seven feet thick.

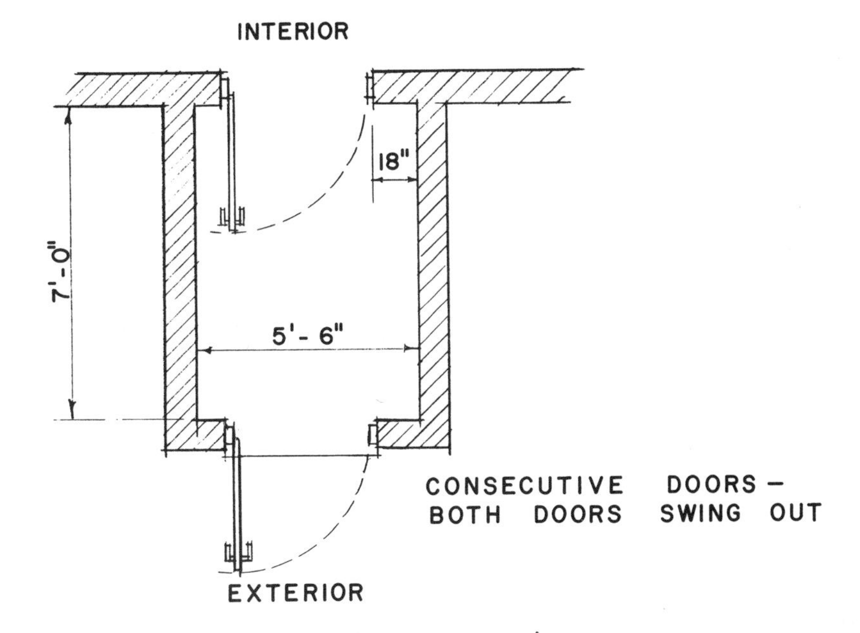

FIGURE 15: AIR LOCK ENTRY

	Ceiling	Wall	Floor
	38	19	22
	33	19	22
	30	19	19
	26	19	13
	26	13	11
	19	11	11

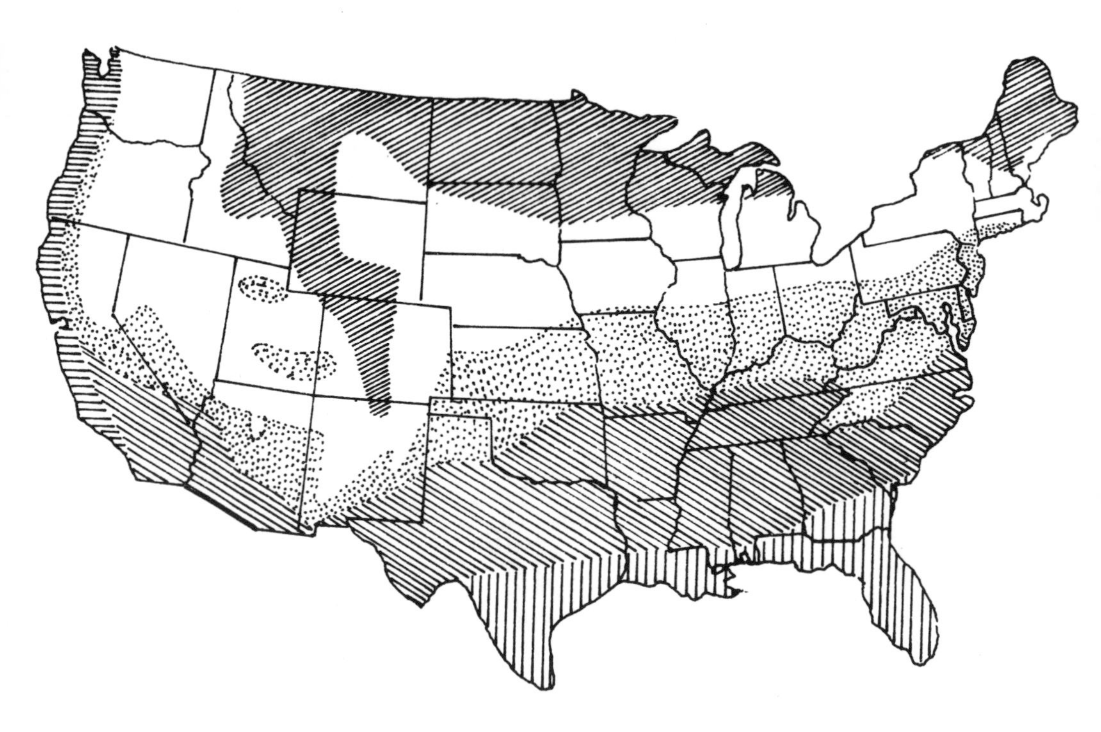

Figure 16: Regional Insulation R-Value Recommendations

The amount of insulation needed depends on such factors as climate, materials used, area to be insulated, and method of installation. Obviously, colder climates need more insulation in the winter and warmer climates need more insulation in the summer. (See chart in fig. 16 for recommendations.) Since various insulating materials have differing R-values per inch, one should think in terms of achieving the recommended R-value rather than thinking only of the thickness of the material installed. In the process of insulating a building, the area that should be given priority is the area where the greatest heat loss occurs. Usually, this is the ceiling because the temperature differential is greatest at this point. However, significant heat loss will occur at exterior walls and at the floor, so these areas should also be adequately insulated. Proper installation of insulating materials is critical in achieving maximum thermal performance. Gaps and open spaces between insulation will create thermal paths for heat flow that can seriously reduce the R-value in the area involved.

Shading.—One of the primary causes of heat gain in a building is direct sunlight through windows. Shading is one of the most effective methods of controlling this passive solar gain. Wide roof overhangs, horizontal building projections, and vertical fins on the building can sometimes be designed to block the direct rays of the summer sun. This may be especially important for south- and west-facing windows in areas that are used all during the week. These windows will be the source of significant heat gain in the summer if they are not shaded in some manner.

Energy-Efficient Mechanical Systems

Heating, ventilating, and air-conditioning systems for churches should be designed with special attention to the particular schedule of church services and activities. Too often, systems are designed for churches just as they would be for office buildings, schools, or industries. That may be a wise solution when churches operate on the same schedule as these other entities. However, suppose the church uses its buildings only two days a week. That may dictate an altogether different system. Therefore, church leaders should be certain those involved in designing the mechanical system are fully aware of the church's usual schedule.

Comprehensive studies of the relative costs of different energy sources would be helpful. These studies should deal also with the future availability of proposed fuel sources. They should include some evaluation of the impact of projected market conditions for these fuels. If heat pumps are considered, give special attention to the effects of electric demand charges and to an energy management system that will allow the demand to be controlled. The high-demand charges now being billed make these controls imperative. Churches also need to investigate possible savings available through off-peak rate schedules. Most electric utilities now offer attractive savings to customers who can use most of their electricity at off-peak hours. Many churches are prime candidate for these lower rates because they use more electricity during off-peak hours.

To this point, churches have done little to explore possible savings through thermal storage systems. However, large churches with extensive weekday programs and ministries may need to carefully consider some of these possibilities. Any serious consideration should be based on through engineering studies that document costs and projected savings.

Zone for flexible use and control.—Most churches would profit from a system that allows them to condition only those areas needed for particular services and activities. If the entire facility must be conditioned anytime part of it is needed, significant energy will be wasted. Therefore, the following areas should be on separate systems or zones:

- Offices
- Library
- Conference room or committee meeting room
- Day-care facilities
- Fellowship hall
- Areas of the building needed for Wednesday night activities
- Music rehearsal space

Separate zones or systems for these areas will involve more expense in the initial installation, but the annual operational savings will be significant. The extra installation costs should be recovered through reduced operating costs within four to five years. Unless the zoning provisions are made in the initial installation, the cost of making them later may be prohibitive.

Install adequate controls.—Adequate controls will vary according to the size of the church and the type mechanical system installed. Small churches with oil or gas hot-air furnaces may need only simple controls such as seven-day clocks. These clocks allow for programmed operations for starting and stopping the mechanical systems for each day of the week. Even small churches that install heat pumps will profit from the installation of small microprocessors that go several steps beyond seven-day clock capabilities. Additionally, they monitor temperature changes and adjust the start-up time as needed to properly condition the building for the programmed time.

Churches installing hot-water boilers should consult with qualified professionals in the field so that the latest in controls will be installed. Controls such as the following should be evaluated for installation.

• *Boiler-reset controller*—This adjusts the water temperature in the boiler in relation to outside temperature, thus allowing the boiler to operate more efficiently.

• *Demand-control switch*—This keeps the boiler off until a thermostat in the building calls for heat. Therefore, during long periods when no heat is needed in the building the boiler does not operate. Caution: a freeze-override switch should be installed with this control to prevent freeze damage when the demand control switch has the boiler off.

Many churches need energy management systems that allow them to control electric demand by load leveling, phasing, and load shedding. The systems are available with varying levels of sophistication ranging all the way from simple settings to telephone-command control. Churches need professional assistance in the design of a system adequate for their needs. The system should not be overdesigned or so complex it will not be properly used by the church. In most instances, a church will profit by having a professional who is not a vendor design the system. With his design specifications, bids can be obtained from various vendors. In this way, a church is more likely to get a system that fully meets their needs and is not overdesigned with features the church is not likely to use effectively.

Purchase Energy-Efficient Equipment

If a church is to be a good steward of energy consumption, it will need to purchase equipment designed for energy-efficient operation. This includes all energy-consuming equipment: mechanical, kitchen, lighting fixtures, and water heaters. Manufacturers must now rate equipment with an energy-efficient rating (EER). This allows the purchaser to compare the projected operating cost of the items involved.

Special attention should be given to equipment that will use the greatest amount of energy. In most instances, this will be the heating and air-conditioning equipment. Boilers and furnaces that are gas- or oil-fired are now available with a high-efficiency rating. They will be more expensive than units with a lower fuel-efficiency rating, but the money saved in operating costs over the first several years will more than make up for the difference. Purchasing the cheapest equipment may be not only false economy but also a violation of Christian stewardship principles.

Working with Limited Funds for Energy Conservation

Most churches have limited funds with which to provide for energy efficiency. Therefore, committees need to do their homework, consult with the best professional expertise available, and do actual payback studies to discover how to make the best investment of these funds. One general principle to follow is to install items that have extremely high retrofitting costs and delay items that can be easily and inexpensively installed later. For example, a building with a cathedral ceiling should have adequate insulation on the decking. If this is not installed initially, the church will probably have to wait until a new roof is installed fifteen or twenty years later.

Another example is an energy management system that gives maximum control over peak electrical use. The cost of installing this system during construction is much less than the cost of adding it after the building is completed. In fact, waiting for a later installation may limit its flexibility. In that case, the church may have completely lost the opportunity to obtain maximum energy-efficient operations. Committees should consult with professionals to identify those items that cannot be delayed without undue financial costs later.

Maintenance Efficiency

Building committees should give attention to much more than initial construction costs. They also should be concerned with the kind of building that can be maintained over the years without undue maintenance problems and costs. This applies to both the building's exterior and interior. What seems at first consideration to be the least expensive construction may turn out to be the most expensive to maintain. Thus, what is saved in construction costs can quickly be expended for maintenance. If these maintenance costs must be repeated over and over, the church will be saddled with unnecessary financial obligation for years to come.

Therefore, committees need to consider life-cycle cost analysis. This analysis factors construction costs and maintenance costs together and compares them with similar data from other alternatives. Through such a study, a committee may discover that after a few years the church will be better off financially with the more expensive product or the more durable material. However, it is also a fallacy to assume that the more expensive product is always more efficient. There is no adequate substitute for life-cycle cost analysis studies.

Maintenance of mechanical equipment is important. Therefore, the church may consider awarding the mechanical subcontract to a firm that will be both capable and available to provide quality maintenance for the equipment. Usually, this means the firm should be located within a reasonable distance of the church. Few problems with a new building are as troublesome as the chronic malfunction of heating and air-conditioning equipment.

Concerns for maintenance efficiency are important, but they must not become the overriding issues dictating design and materials. There are sometimes valid and compelling theological reasons for some decisions related to materials and design. Where these exist, the church should not hesitate to make the needed investment. The primary concern is to construct a building that meets theological and functional criteria, not to produce the least expensive facility.

9

Providing Program Accessibility for All Persons

Governmental surveys indicate at least thirty-six million persons in the United States have limited mobility due to physical handicaps. Leaders in organizations who serve disabled persons think that estimate is low. They estimate there may be as many as eighty-five million people in this country with a physical disability. Since disability is defined in different ways, more precise estimates are difficult to obtain. But these figures, coupled with the exploding senior adult population and their sometimes limited mobility, make it important to provide for all persons in church facilities.

Federal, state, and local laws now require buildings and programs to be accessible so that all persons can participate at the level of their choice. Because of compliance with these accessibility codes and standards, many buildings are now designed so handicapped persons can participate as other members of the community. As a result, handicapped persons are more independent, free to make more personal choices, and free to participate in more outside activities.

Many churches have responded in good faith to these codes and provided at least limited accessibility. However, the church should not be content to meet minimal code requirements. The church should be a leading advocate and its facilities a model for program accessibility. This means the church should make it possible for those with handicaps to participate in any program the church offers.

Some states have taken rather bold steps and now require handicapped access to such areas as the platform and the choir. This is not always easy to achieve architecturally. However, the church dare not turn its back on millions of handicapped persons by refusing to open the way for their full participation in its life and work. The church should not communicate an attitude of indifference toward persons with limited mobility and other difficulties. If church facilities bar these persons from participation, what message is the church sending them?

Those needing special facility considerations are the visually impaired, those with hearing disabilities, those with limited mobility, and persons in wheelchairs and on crutches. Church facilities should be designed to be user friendly to all persons. Parking lots, entrances, corridors, and other spaces can be designed to communicate sensitivity and concern for all persons. From the moment people drive onto the property to the time they arrive at their activity, the facilities should indicate, "We were designed with you in mind."

Parking

- Handicapped spaces should be near a major entrance that provides ground-level access or a ramp.
- Pavement should be level if possible.
- Parking spaces should be located so that persons using braces, crutches, or wheelchairs do not have to move into driveways behind parked cars. Direct access to the building should be available from the front of the vehicle.
- Parking spaces should be a minimum of ten feet wide with four feet between spaces for wheelchairs (see fig. 17).
- Parking spaces for the handicapped should be marked with appropriate signs.

Walks and Ramps

- Walks should be a minimum of four feet wide.
- Sloped walks and ramps should be used for changes in elevation. Maximum slope of walks with no handrails required is 5 percent—one foot rise in twenty feet.
- Walks that slope should blend into a common level when crossing other walks or driveways.
- Ramps should slope not more than 8.33 percent—one foot in twelve (see fig. 18).

• Surfaces for walks and ramps should be nonslip. Broom-finished concrete, Carborundum, or rubber make good surfaces.

• Ramps should have a 3-foot level platform at thirty-foot intervals for safety and rest (see fig. 19).

• At the top of the ramp there should be a 5′ × 5′ level platform. The ramp should be located so there is an 18-inch wall space (some codes require 24 inches) on the exterior side the door handle is on (see fig. 20).

• Ramps that slope more than 5 percent should have a handrail on one side.

• Handrails should be continuous, smooth, and extend one foot beyond the bottom and top of the ramp or turned at right angles where necessary. Handrails should be installed 30-34 inches above the surface of the ramp (see fig. 21).

• If a ramp drops off on either side, handrails are required.

• A level platform is required where a ramp turns.

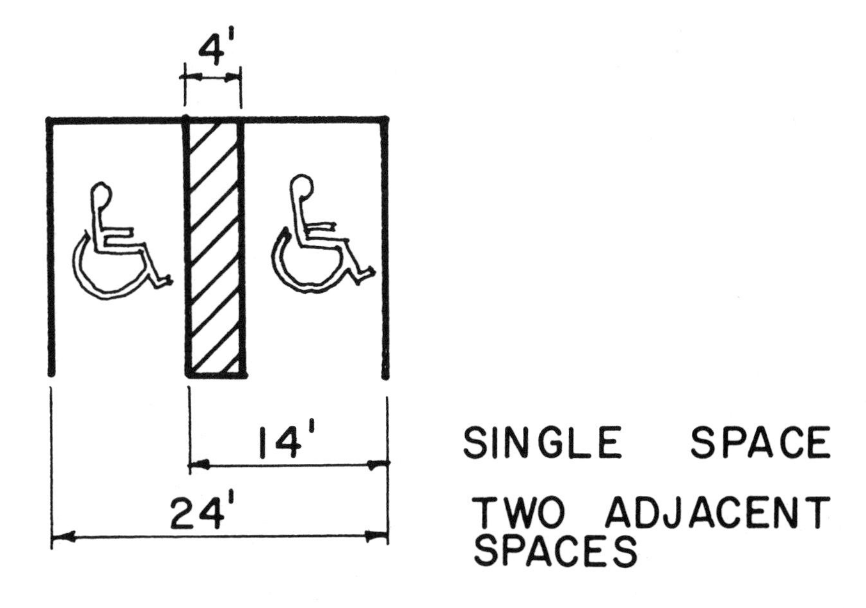

FIGURE 17: HANDICAPPED PARKING

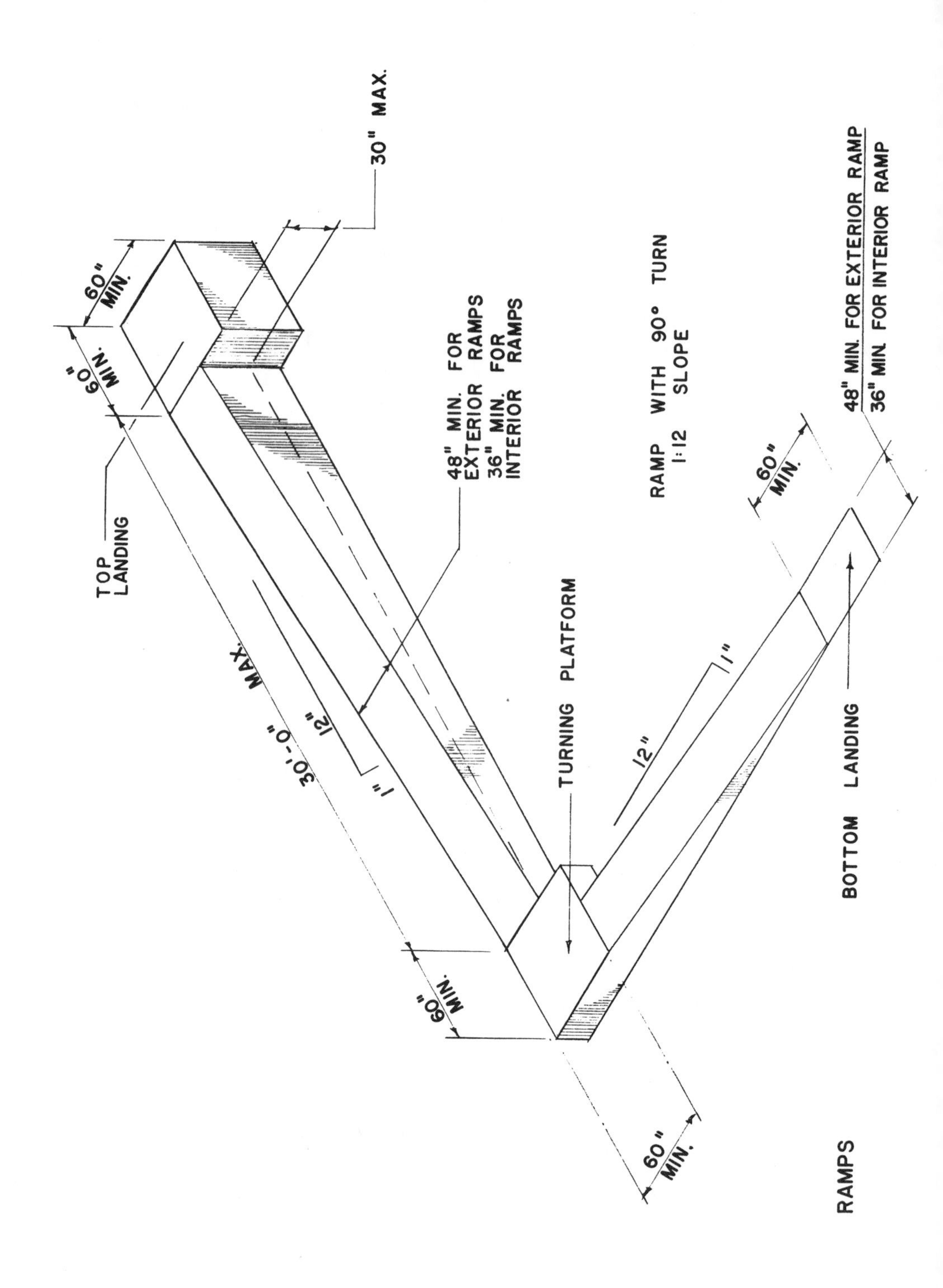

Figure 18: Handicapped Ramp Dimensions

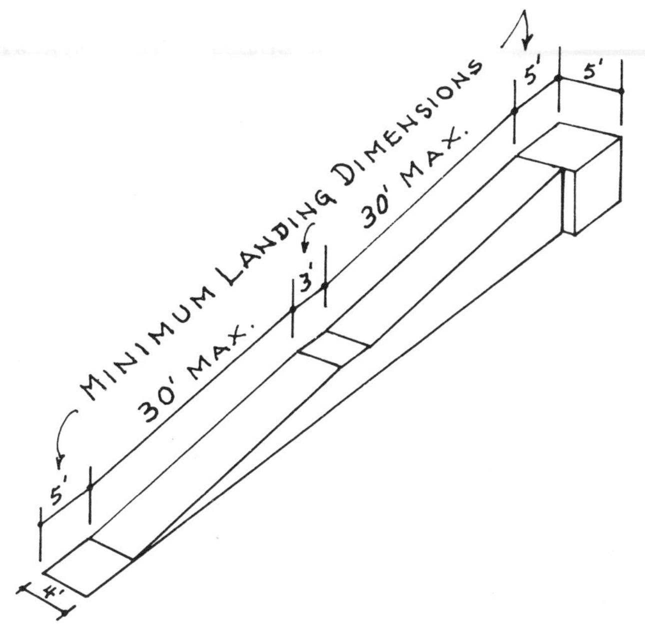

FIGURE 19: STRAIGHT RUN RAMP DIMENSIONS

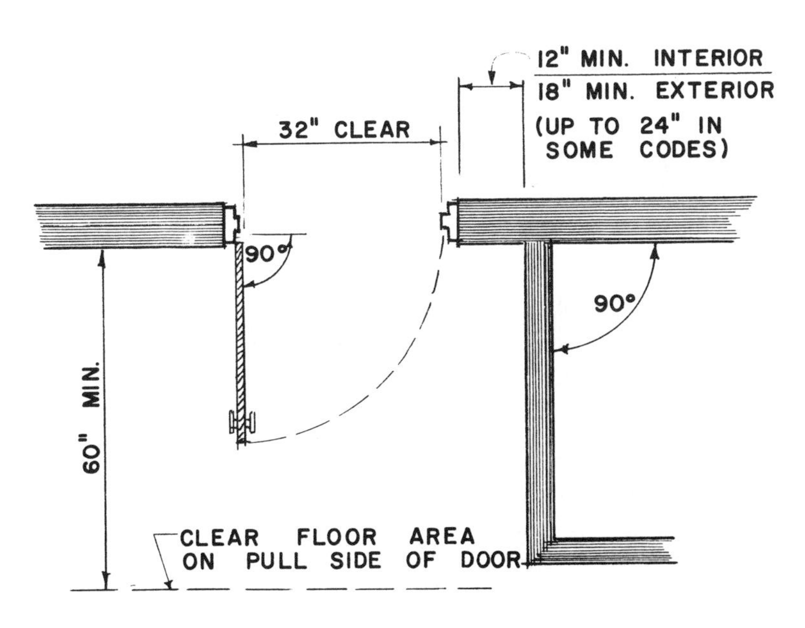

FIGURE 20: HANDICAPPED-ACCESSIBLE DOORWAY

Entrances

• There should be no threshold step.

• An unobstructed opening of at least 2′ 8″ is required. When double doors are used, one of them must meet this requirement.

• Doors must operate with a single effort.

• The floor on the inside and outside of an exit door must be level for a distance of five feet. The level area should extend one foot beyond the hinge side of the door.

• Thresholds at doors should be beveled and have a maximum thickness of ¾ of an inch.

• Framed glass doors should have a bottom rail or a protector strip at least 7.5 inches high to serve as a push rail for wheelchair bumpers.

• The pressure required to open doors should be not more than fifteen pounds.

• Airlocks should have a minimum of seven feet between the doors to allow for easy wheelchair passage.

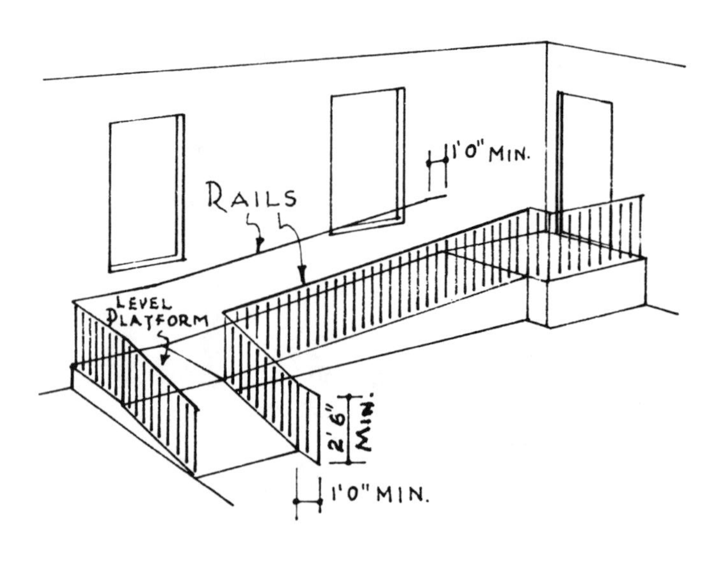

FIGURE 21: RAMP HANDRAILS

Designing the Interior for the Handicapped

Unfortunately, many churches have limited their concern to accessibility to the building. Too little thought has been given to the needs of the handicapped inside the facility. Many interior features can restrict the handicapped and make it difficult for them to function. For example, the following conditions can create real problems for the handicapped: changes in floor levels where there are no ramps, small rest rooms, narrow corridors, wall switches that are too high, doors that are too narrow, and no place for wheelchairs in the worship center.

An average-size person in a wheelchair has an average vertical reach of 60 inches, an average horizontal reach of 30.8 inches, and the average diagonal reach, as to a light switch, is to a point 48 inches above the floor. This data is helpful in designing the building interior (see fig. 22). Care must also be taken to design handicapped-accessible drinking fountains (see fig. 23).

Corridors

• A minimum width of five feet is required for two individuals in wheelchairs to pass each other.

• The minimum width for two persons on crutches to pass each other in a corridor is five feet six inches.

• For a person to turn a wheelchair around, a minimum corridor width is 60 inches.

• There should be no steps in a corridor. Ramps should be provided to connect different floor levels.

• Only nonslip floor surfaces should be installed.

Stairs and Elevators

• Handrails should be installed 30-34 inches above steps, and at least one handrail should extend a minimum of 12 inches beyond the top and bottom steps (see fig. 24).

• Stair treads should have rounded or slanted nosing so as not to provide a ledge where crutches or braces can hang and trip people (see fig. 25).

• Handrails should be designed to provide an easy and secure grip (see fig. 24).

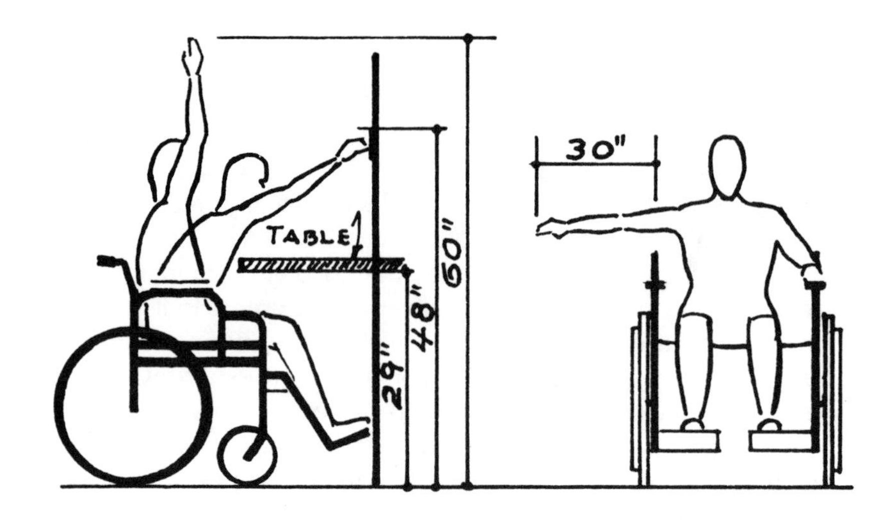

FIGURE 22: AVERAGE REACH FROM WHEELCHAIR

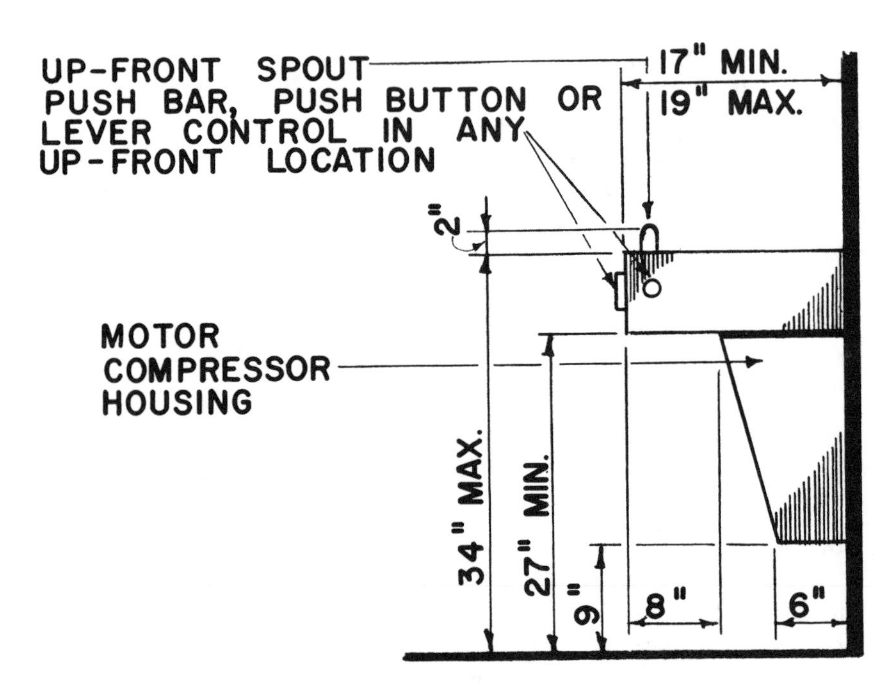

FIGURE 23: WALL-MOUNTED DRINKING FOUNTAIN
FOR HANDICAPPED

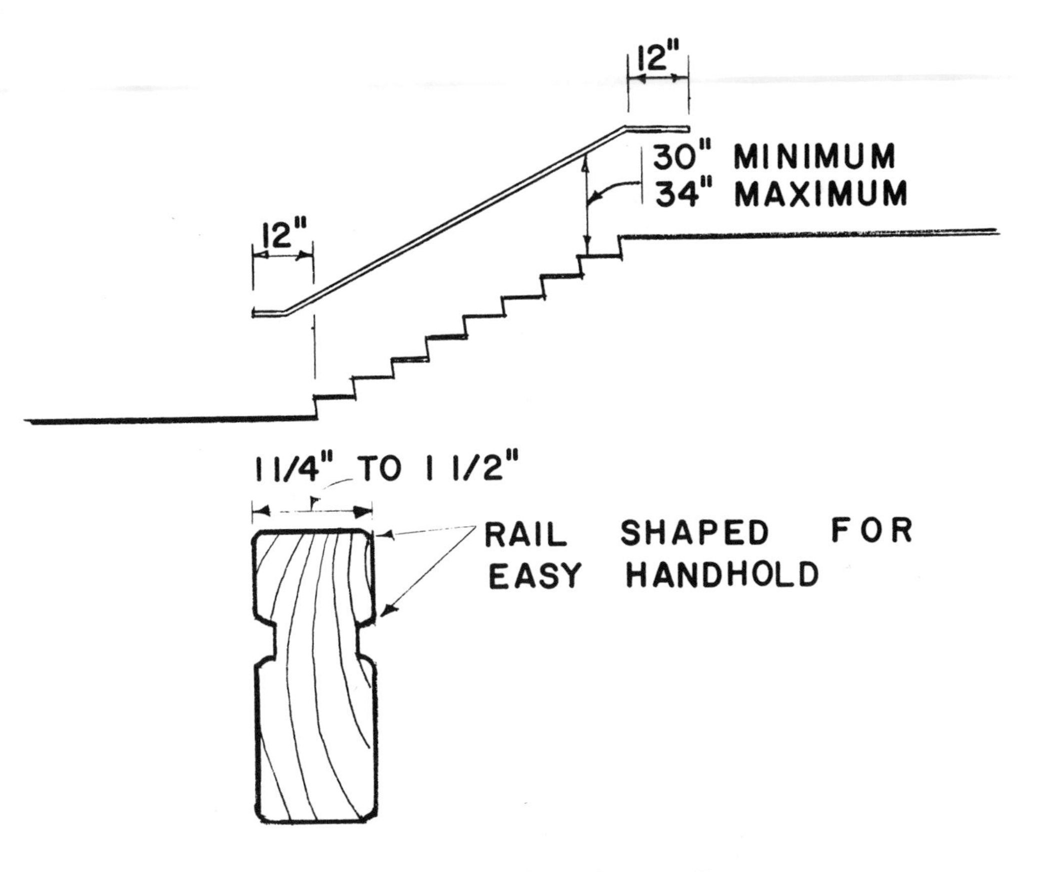

Figure 24: Stair And Ramp Handrail Details

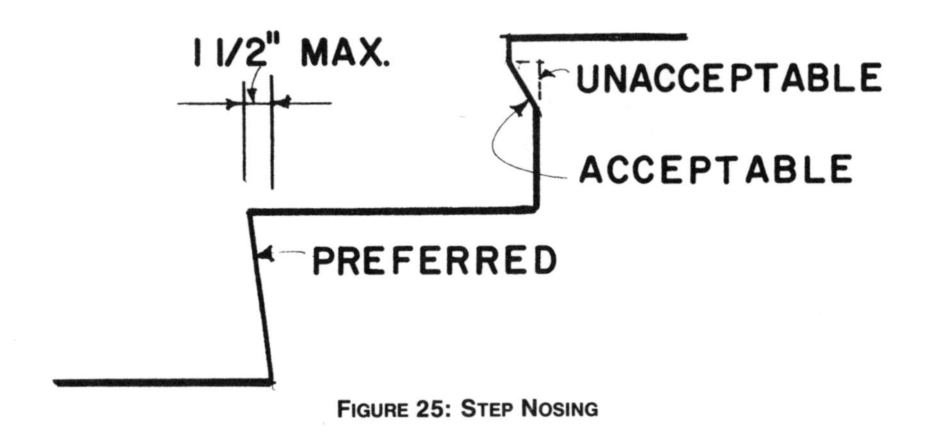

Figure 25: Step Nosing

MINIMUM SIZES AND CAPACITIES FOR ELEVATORS

BUILDING 3 STORIES OR LESS	A = 68"	B = 51"
MINIMUM CAPACITY	2,000 POUNDS	

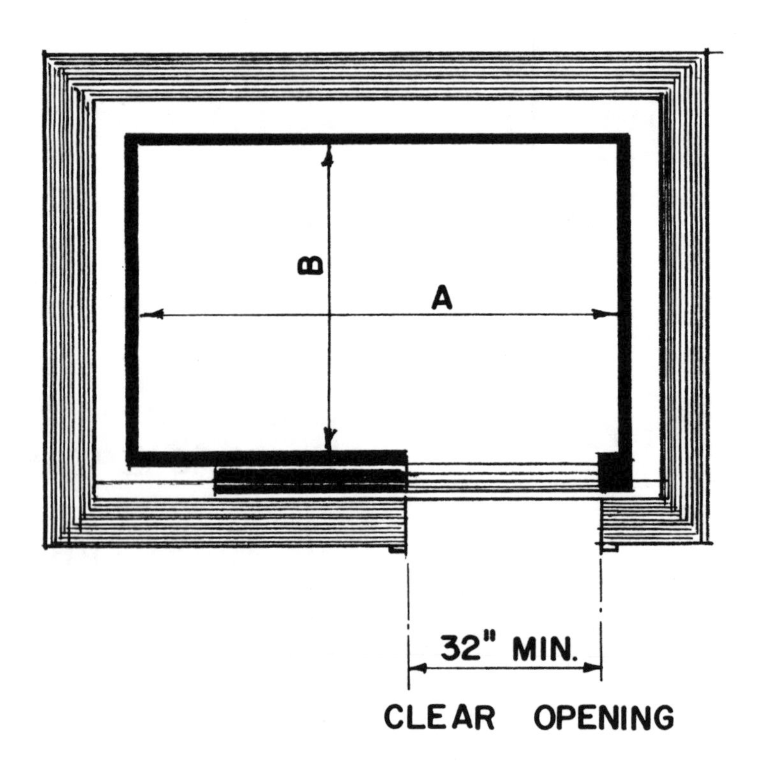

FIGURE 26: ELEVATOR

• Elevators are now required in many areas for all multilevel buildings. Even if codes do not require them, they are still a wise investment. (See fig. 26 for minimum size.) An elevator can open all upper floors to events and activities that would otherwise need to be located on ground level. When churches consider a fifty-year building utilization, the annual cost of an elevator is extremely reasonable. Even if the church does not install the elevator during construction, it would be wise to provide an elevator tower for future installation.

Rest Rooms

• Where rest rooms are located, at least one men's room and one women's room on each floor must have one of each type fixture accessible to the physically handicapped.

• Clear floor space must be designed five feet by five feet to allow for wheelchair turning (see figs. 27-30).

• At least one men's room and one women's room shall have one stall at least 3 feet wide and 6 feet deep with a clear door opening of not less than 32 inches and a door that swings out. The stall shall have a water closet with the seat 16.5 inches to 19.5 inches above the floor and grab bars on both sides 33 inches high and 54 inches long. Grab bars shall be 1 ¼ inches or 1.5 inches outside diameter and be mounted 1.5 inches from the wall (see figs. 27-30).

• Minimum clear dimensions in front of the stall must be 3 feet by 3 feet, 6 inches.

• One lavatory shall be provided with a 29-inch clearance from the bottom of the apron to the floor. The top of the lavatory shall be a minimum of 34 inches above floor level.

• One wall-mounted urinal not more than 19 inches high or one floor-type urinal shall be provided in the men's room.

• Towel dispensers, trash disposal units, and other equipment should be mounted with operating mechanism no more than 40 inches above floor level.

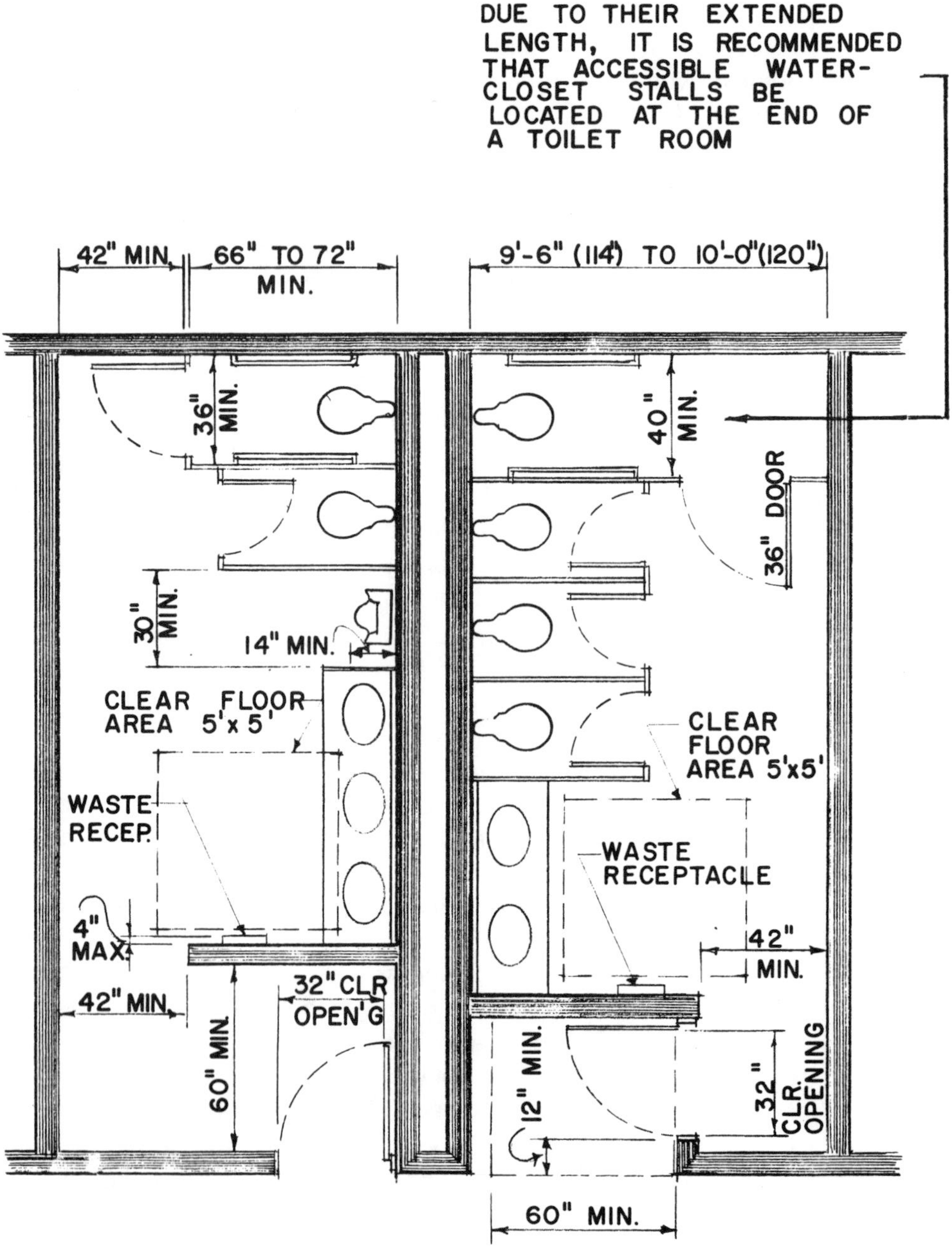

Figure 27: Group Toilet Floor Plan

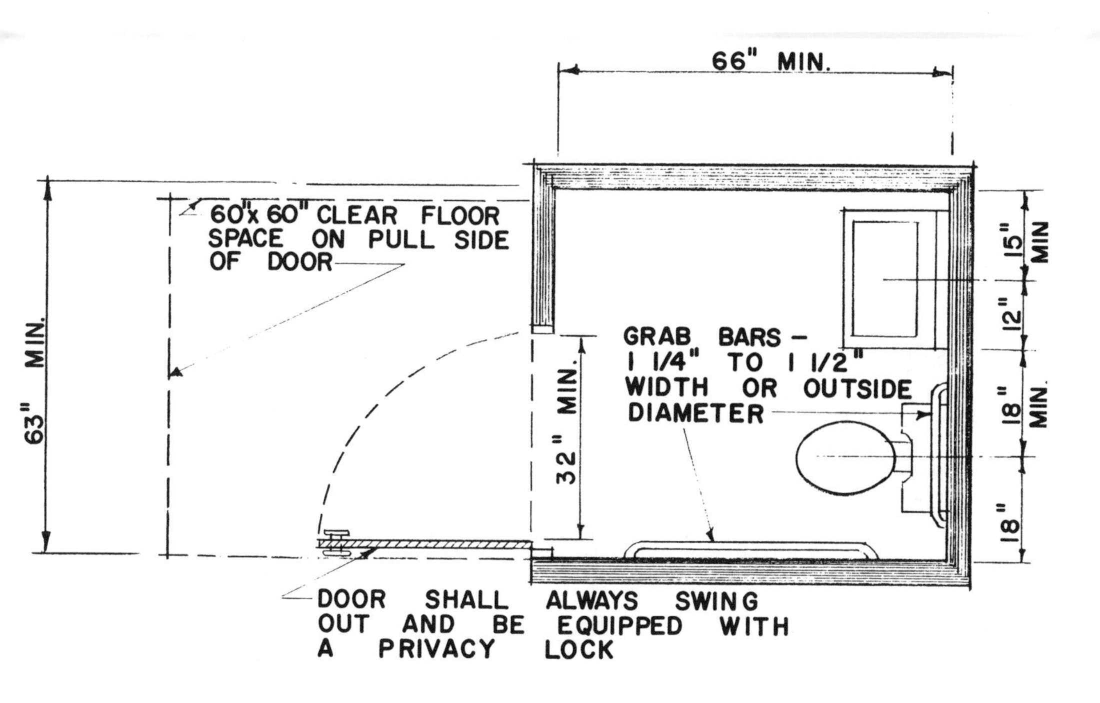

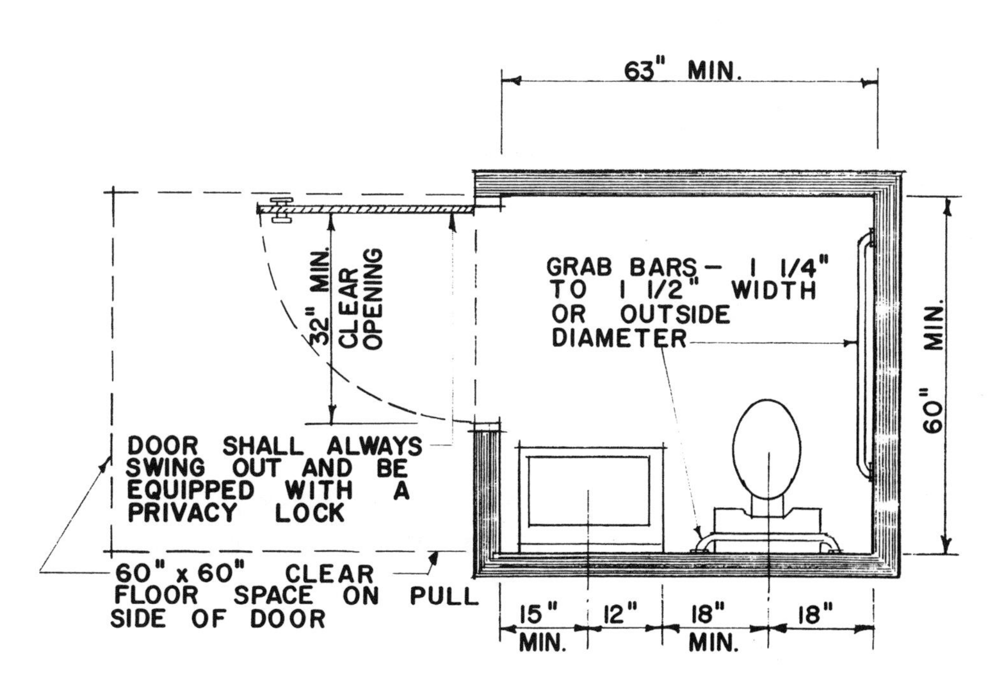

Figure 28: Individual Toilet Rooms

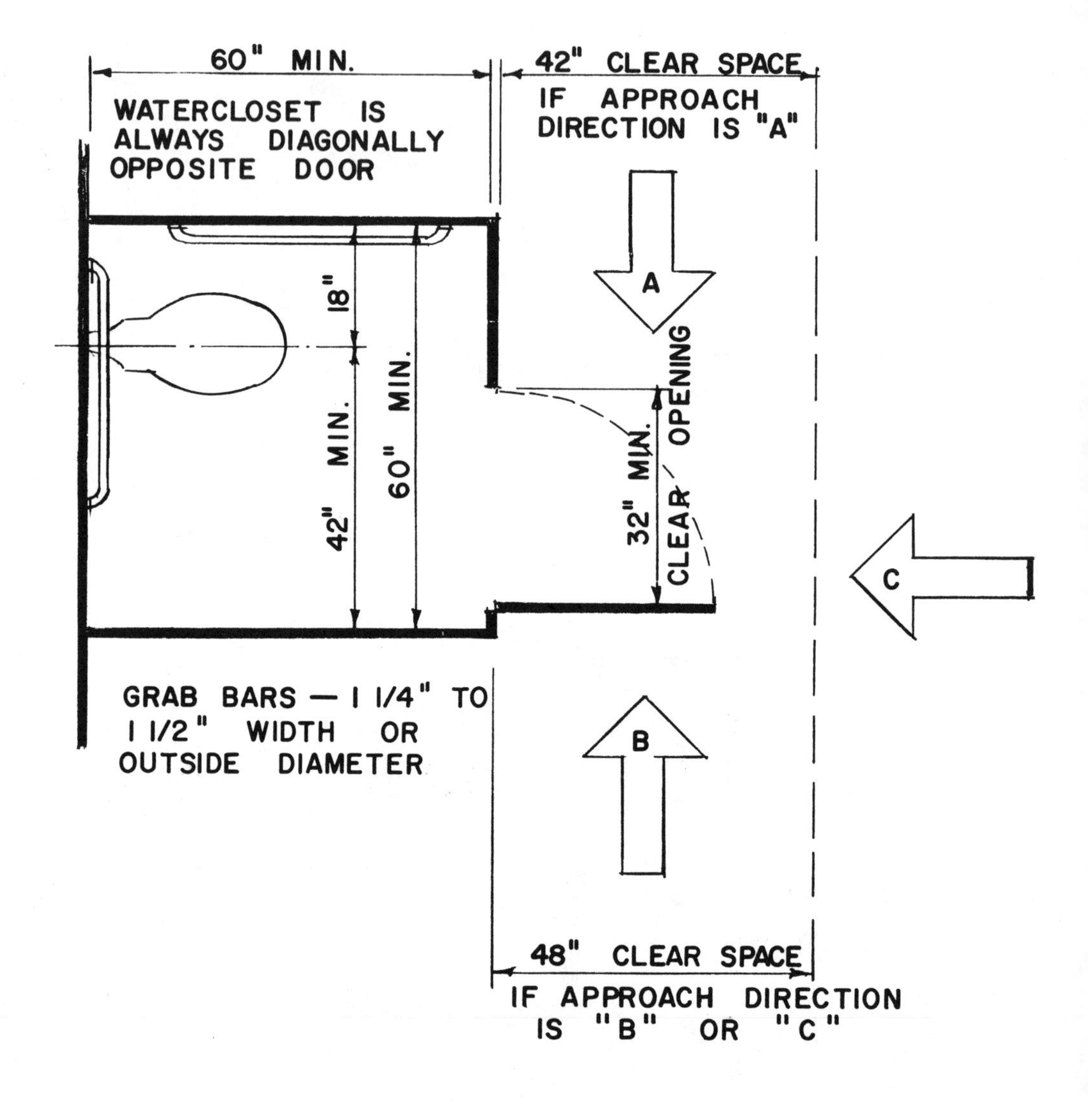

Figure 29: Large Handicapped-Accessible Stall

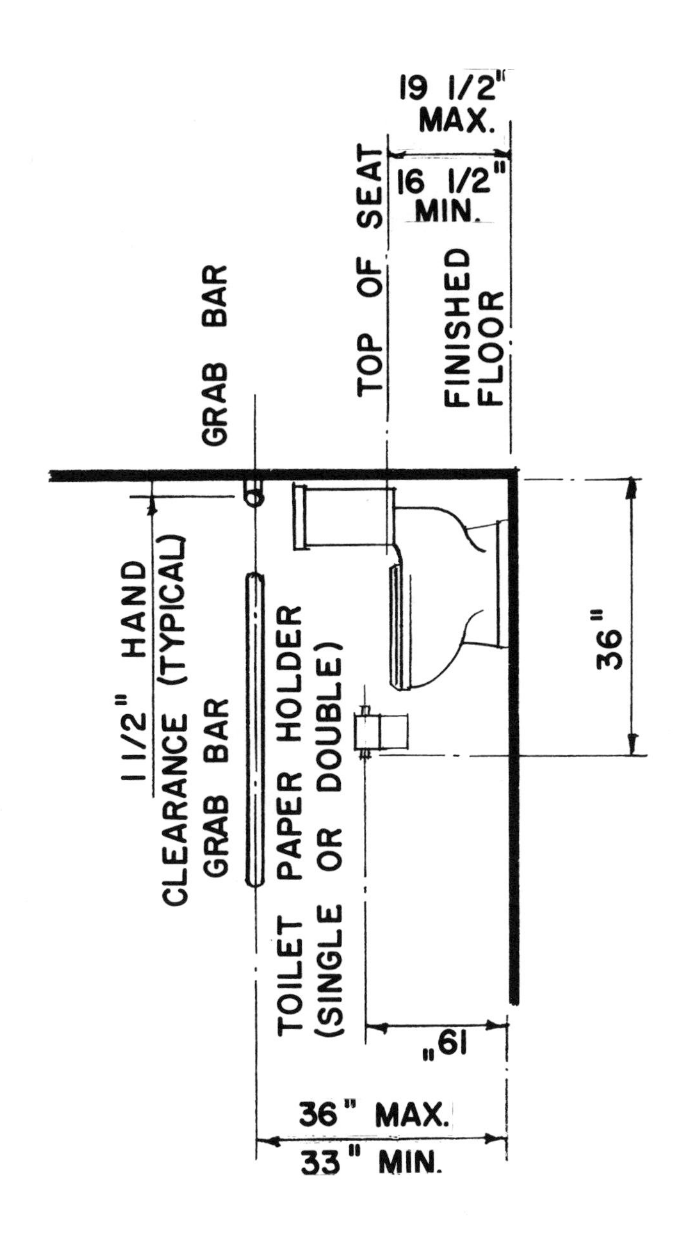

Figure 30: Elevation Of Handicapped-Accessible Toilet

Check Local Codes

The national handicapped accessibility code is provided by the American National Standards, Incorporated (ANSI), but some states have compiled and published their own code. Codes continually change and expand. The information and illustrations given in this book will need to be checked against the latest code revisions. Therefore, the committee should see that local codes are checked to determine the standards required.

10

Choosing the System to Deliver the Building

After months of study, evaluation, planning, and design work, the building-steering committee finally comes to the time for construction. Up to this point the process may have seemed like a series of frustrations. Now that it's time for construction, the committee may feel they can breath a sigh of relief. The dream is about to be fulfilled before their eyes. But hold on a moment. Don't assume from this point on all will go according to schedule and budget. It probably will not. In fact, some of the major frustrations may come during construction. The committee does not simply select a contractor, sign a contract, and then take a vacation. Major committee responsibilities occur during the construction phase. So, summon your courage and renew your determination for this last major push toward the realization of the building dream.

Evaluate Systems for Delivering the Building

An informed committee will not wait until the construction documents are completed to explore options for the construction process. Long before that time they should familiarize themselves with various systems designed to actually deliver the completed building. In recent years, there has been a proliferation of delivery systems for construction projects. The committee needs to know enough about these systems to be able to evaluate the advantages and disadvantages of each.

Traditional Approach

The traditional approach to designing and constructing a building begins with the selection of an architect who develops construction documents. This is followed by the bidding process—a time when general contractors submit bids for constructing the building according to the construction documents. Then, the contract is awarded—usually to the low bidder. There are a number of variations and adaptations of the traditional approach.

Advantages

1. The church selects and employs the architect who is directly responsible to the church for the design of the building and usually for specific construction-administration tasks.

2. With adequately detailed construction documents, contractors do not have to guess at the level of quality and quantity and, therefore, can submit bids for the construction of the project. Competitive bidding should secure the lowest contract price for the building as designed. The building should be constructed according to specifications and at the contract price. (Insurance and bonding provide additional protection for the church.)

3. This method provides for significant checks and balances. The architect is the church's representative to assure that the construction documents are followed, shop drawings approved, all change orders detailed and credited, and a comprehensive final inspection conducted.

Disadvantages

1. Early estimates of construction costs often lack precision. Final cost of the project cannot be known until bids are obtained. If the bids are significantly over budget, it may be difficult to revise the plans to bring the cost down. Professional estimators are available who, for a fee, will make a cost estimate before plans are complete and with time for changes before bidding. Usually they "guarantee" their estimates to be within 2 to 5 percent of actual costs. These estimators often are not used because the architect does not want to absorb the added cost and the committee does not see the importance of this kind of input at this point.

2. Since the architect does not know who the general contractor will be, the construction documents may not be developed to take full advantage of the most cost-effective systems, materials,

and details. Of course, numerous factors interplay in this process. The architect must keep in mind the unity of the design. Changing materials often has a domino effect and changing one detail may lead to changes in several other areas.

3. The nature of this arrangement often allows both the architect and the committee to bypass significant financial disciplines that could lead them to adopt firm and realistic budget parameters. Therefore, both the architect and the committee may contribute to the development of plans that are beyond the financial capability of the church.

If they will take the time, architects can develop relationships with suppliers and subcontractors who can help compare alternate materials, equipment, and assemblies. Often architects rely on published data or data from previous projects that establish a projected cost per square foot. This may not take into account the uniqueness or new aspects of the current project. Architects and owners are seldom aware of developments that will precipitate construction cost increases. Contractors anticipate such things as the possible impact of trade-union contracts, shipping costs, and other economic indicators.

There are, of course, ways to minimize the disadvantages of the traditional system. The negotiated contract is one way. This approach brings a general contractor into the process during the design phase and draws on his expertise in many areas that affect construction costs. The contractor can often supply firm cost estimates for various alternatives. Therefore, the architect and the committee can be kept aware of the financial impact of their decisions.

The negotiated contact is a means by which the committee, in consultation with the architect, selects a contractor on a negotiated basis. The basis may be either one or a combination of the following:

- Construction costs plus either a fixed fee or a percentage of the cost of construction;
- A guaranteed maximum cost, which includes the contractor's fee, with incentives paid to the contractor for any savings under the maximum cost.

This arrangement brings the architect, the contractor, and the committee together as a team. Each member of the team has a significant part in keeping the project within the accepted budget parameters. Team members must accept their individual responsibility in the process. Too often, the committee blames the architect or the contractor for excessive costs.

One of the problems with a negotiated contract may be the lack of competitive bidding. That can be dealt with through a process of prequalifying contractors during the design phase. These contractors agree to consult with the committee and the architect through the design process to achieve some of the advantages of the negotiated contract in a competitive bid environment. In return, these contractors are given the exclusive privilege of bidding on the project, and the lowest bidder is awarded the contract.

Several alternatives to the traditional approach of the design-construction process have emerged. Committees should be aware of these and be able to evaluate the strengths and weaknesses of each. (I am indebted to Fred Turner, senior manager, Architectural Services in the Church Architecture Department of The Sunday School Board of the Southern Baptist Convention, for many of the comparisons of the alternate approaches.)

Design-Build Approach

This approach combines the disciplines of design and construction and brings them into one firm. The goal is to bring together an architect and a contractor who work as a team to provide full services in design and construction. When these two professionals understand and complement each other, significant advantages emerge to produce a well-coordinated project. Generally, design-build firms work with the client to determine in the early stages the broad parameters of the project: scope, structural system, mechanical system, roofing system, materials, finishes, and maximum cost. Design-build firms tend to use standard materials, finishes, and structural systems. In some instances, they specialize in certain types of buildings and construction methods.

Advantages

1. The client has a single source for the delivery of the desired building and does not have to work with two or more firms.

2. The relative benefits and costs of various design alternatives can be evaluated more precisely during the design stage. The owner and design-build firm can then make a decision based on complete data.

3. A firm cost is set at the earliest possible time. This, of course, imposes severe restraints upon the owner because the projected cost is tied directly to the established design parameters. Every change made can increase the cost of the project.

Disadvantages

1. The architect is primarily responsible to the firm and not to the client. For this reason, he may not represent the church's interests as effectively as if he were employed directly by the church.

2. Architectural drawings are usually less than complete. This keeps costs down, but it also gives the design-build firm more latitude in the final product. The result is the church may not get what they expected. In addition, there are usually no (or very few) construction-phase services provided by the architect.

3. Cost control is achieved primarily through manipulation of quality rather than through competition.

4. Too much attention may be given to low initial building costs and life-cycle costing may be sacrificed. This can be a critical mistake that forces a church to pay significant long-term maintenance and operational costs. For example, a focus on low initial building costs can lead to eliminating energy-efficient features that would be cost effective and would be extremely expensive to add later. (See ch. 8 for more details on the wisdom of building energy-efficient structures.)

Construction Management Approach

Construction management was developed primarily for large multimillion dollar projects that needed a coordinator highly skilled in both construction and management. The purpose was twofold:

1. To bring a construction specialist into the design process so he could work with the architect and utilize his construction expertise in early design decisions relating to construction methods, materials, structural systems, and related issues.

2. To bring a person with significant management skills into the construction process for planning, coordination, and execution.

Ideally, the construction manager is employed by the time of the design-development stage or earlier (see ch. 6). He consults with the architect in the design and is responsible for construction of the project. He serves not as the general contractor but as the manager of construction.

Advantages

1. Both the architect and the construction manager are employed by the church and responsible to it.

2. Construction expertise is available to the architect and the committee in the design process.

3. Early construction cost estimates can influence the design of the building and contribute to budget control.

4. Competitive subcontractor bidding can help control costs.

Disadvantages

1. The cost of the construction manager can exceed the savings on a small or medium-size project.

2. Some construction managers and architects do not work well together. This can create conflicts entangling the committee and complicating the entire process. On some projects this conflict has pushed the cost of construction even higher.

3. Bonding and insurance arrangements are more complex than with the traditional approach.

Committees should be aware that some companies use the term "construction management" to designate services that differ significantly from those just described. These companies mix some of the concepts from design-build and construction management. In reality, they offer little more than project supervision but they call it "construction management." (Note this term is in quotation marks, suggesting it has a different meaning from the way the writer has been using it.)

Sometimes they have an agreement with an architect to do a minimum amount of design work for the project. The firm then secures bids from subcontractors and sends in a building superintendent to oversee construction. The superintendent's expertise in construction may be limited, and he may have no skills at all in management.

The company does not guarantee a maximum cost for the project. It obtains subcontract bids and then estimates other costs. Sometimes the firm will talk about a guaranteed cost estimate, and committees usually hear this as if it were a firm contract price. However, it is not. Usually, the contract gives no guarantee that the building will be constructed for a fixed price. If the superintendent makes mistakes and there are cost overruns, the church has to absorb them.

On one project, a building superintendent made a mistake and poured the floor for a large worship center at the wrong elevation. As a result, the church had to build a retaining wall and reroute a sewer line to the other side of the block. The "construction management" firm accepted no liability for these mistakes, even though their superintendent was clearly at fault. The contract with the church was written in such a way that the company avoided all liability.

Another church used a "construction management" firm and was disappointed in some of the workmanship. They tried to secure adjustments and failed. When they explored their options for legal action, they discovered the contract obligated the company to "consult and advise with the church on the construction project." The committee was surprised to learn that was the limit of the company's obligation to the church. The committee remembered all the sales talk and had understood the contract on that basis. They made the mistake of signing a contract without adequate study and evaluation and without legal counsel.

In the interest of objectivity, committees should note that many churches have used "construction management" firms—even those whose expertise is open to question—and been pleased with the result. However, the advantages and disadvantages cited above for construction management do not apply to all firms who call themselves "construction managers." Committees should thoroughly investigate all firms, understand the limits of their services, and submit proposed contracts to an attorney for approval before signing them. Always remember that the sales presentation is not the contract. Verbal understandings are significant only when supported by specific contractual agreements. Remember, too, that terminology does not always mean the same thing to different people. Positive, descriptive terms can be taken over and used for services that may be considerably less professional than the original terms indicated.

Package Builders

These firms offer a church a complete building package: design, construction, and sometimes even furnishings and financing. In some respects these firms are like design-build firms in that one source provides the design and construction work. Package builders usually have an inventory of building packages that have been produced for other churches. They also have a working agreement with an architect to do minor revisions and adaptations. In many instances, the packages are low-cost structures that are produced by cutting corners to reduce the final price. Little or no attention may be given to the church's specific program needs, growth opportunities, long term master-site planning, or to projected operational and maintenance costs.

Package builders offer a variety of working agreements with churches. Some give a firm contract price and bring in their own crews to do the construction work. Others provide only supervision and general administration of the contract and finances. In some instances, the church serves as its own contractor and assumes all the risks usually assumed by the general contractor.

Advantages

1. The church works with only one company.
2. Specialization in a type of building sometimes provides more economical construction.
3. Reliable cost estimates for the project are usually available in the early stages of planning. Therefore, if the church limits itself to the package offered, the final cost should be known very early.

Disadvantages

1. The church gets a standard, stock solution instead of one designed to meet its specific needs. This may mean program needs and future growth possibilities are completely ignored.

2. The architect is secured by the firm and may feel little or no accountability to the church. In many instances, he never goes to the site, never meets with the committee, and has no personal communication with its members.

3. The church may have to assume the same risks a general contractor would.

By now the reader may be thoroughly confused. Which really is the best approach to the challenge of designing and constructing church buildings? The committee must struggle with this question. Members should thoroughly explore the options, evaluate the advantages and disadvantages of each, and determine just what risks they are prepared to recommend their church take. The committee should talk with churches which have used the various alternatives. They should look closely at the buildings constructed by the various systems. They should talk with program leaders about the way the buildings function. They should evaluate the operational and maintenance costs of those buildings. They should obtain legal counsel in evaluating the proposed contract.

After doing all this, the committee will still need to be aware that no approach to the design and construction of buildings is perfect and trouble-free. There will likely be frustrations, disappointments, and failures during the process. There will be delays and bottlenecks along the way. During all these experiences the committee will need to remember its Christian calling to bear witness for Christ. Members should be models of integrity, love, and grace. They should never give the impression that work is more important than a worker or a building more important than the builder. They should relate to the contractor and to all workers as persons who are at the heart of the church's mission.

Choosing a Contractor

No matter which delivery system is selected for construction, some decisions usually have to be made regarding the selection of a contractor or builder. What are some of the issues involved in this selection process?

1. *Select a contractor on the basis of his integrity.*—This is one of the two most important concerns in the process. No matter what other qualifications he possesses, if he lacks integrity, the committee will likely have to fight one battle after another throughout the construction process.

2. *Select a contractor on the basis of competence.*—This ranks in importance with integrity. He should be skilled not only in basic construction techniques but in cost control. He should possess planning and coordination skills so that he can effectively keep the project moving with various subcontractors meeting deadlines. He should be able to monitor and control a complex project.

3. *Select a contractor with a good reputation in the area.*—You want a contractor who has earned respect because of quality work and a sound warranty. The general contractor is the key person in getting subcontractors to stand behind their work. In most instances where a general contractor is used, the church has no formal contract with subcontractors and, therefore, may have little clout with them. However, the general contractor is accountable to the church for the work of the subcontractors. He usually has significant clout with them because of continuing relationships in the construction industry. (The exception to the church's relation to subcontractors occurs when the church has no general contractor and in instances of some "construction management" in which the church has direct contract dealings with the subcontractors.)

Check Points in Selecting a Contractor

1. *Check on the quality of work he has done on other projects.*—This involves not just a visual inspection of those projects but some evaluation from committees and maintenance personnel. Have there been problems in workmanship or materials? Has there been any problem with maintenance?

2. *Check on his track record for meeting schedules and deadlines.*—Is he known as a contractor who keeps a project moving and brings it in on schedule? If your project is not a large

one, will he push other projects in ahead of yours? If a deadline is critical for you, consider the possibility of writing a penalty clause into the contract. This imposes a monetary penalty for every day's delay beyond the scheduled completion date.

3. *Check on his skills in monitoring and controlling costs.*—Even if the church has a firm contract with him, cost-control skills will be important. If his costs begin to exceed his bid, he may start to look for places to cut corners. The result may not be discovered by the committee, but it can certainly affect the quality of the building.

4. *Check on the reliability of his warranty after the building is occupied.*—Reputable contractors stand behind their projects. They are concerned that the buildings be as free of problems as possible. They will schedule return trips to make needed adjustments or repairs. Do not expect the contractor to assume all the responsibility or liability for problems that may occur. In some instances, the problem may be the responsibility of the equipment manufacturer, or it may have been the result of faulty material or design. There are times when the architect, the contractor, and a manufacturer's representative may have to try to resolve a problem.

5. *Secure a performance bond to protect the church in the event of the contractor's default on the project.*—This bond should provide for the completion of the building, including contractor performance, labor, and materials. It also should cover extra work by the architect that is often required when a bonding company must take over a project. Large and reputable contractors have been known to get caught in serious cash flow problems and have to default. A performance bond guarantees that the church will obtain the completed building at the contract price. If there were no performance bond and the contractor defaulted, the church would simply have to pick up the pieces, find a new contractor, and negotiate for the completion of the building. The original contract price would no longer be guaranteed.

The performance, labor, and materials payment bond should be identified in the contract documents and presented in review along with the contractor's bid. The cost of the bond can be broken out of the base bid as an alternate. Even if the church elects not to require a bond on the project, there is wisdom in stipulating that the bond be a part of the contractor's bid. Bonding companies establish premiums on the basis of the perceived risk factor and past performance of the contractors. Therefore, a committee can learn some things about contractors by examining the certified written quotation from the bonding company. This might even alert the committee to some unknown problems or potential risks involved with a particular contractor.

This is an appropriate place to draw attention to the importance of providing adequate insurance during construction. The committee should make certain that proper coverage is provided in each of the following areas:

- Liability
- Builder's risk
- Workman's compensation
- Fire and casualty
- Property damage

Builder's risk insurance coverage may need additional explanation. This is a kind of interim insurance that covers the building as it is being constructed. It protects the contractor and the church against loss until such time as the building can be completed and insured as other church property is insured.

Insurance coverage should be discussed with the architect and the agent who carries the church's insurance on existing structures to be certain there is no needless duplication and that no area is being overlooked.

If a general contractor has the project, the contract will usually specify the coverage he must provide. In most instances, this includes liability, builder's risk, and workmen's compensation insurance. Other delivery systems present varying degrees of complex insurance coverage because the lines of liability and financial responsibility are often not as clearly drawn as with a general contractor. Some of these delivery systems place all of the responsibility on the church. Committees should be absolutely certain that adequate coverage is provided for the church.

The liabilities and risks are too great to cut corners and leave the church unprotected during this critical time.

Give Careful Attention to the Contract

The church will be wise to use the American Institute of Architects' construction contract with the contractor. This contract represents recognized industry standards; has clear, legal language; and holds no hidden clauses or bias. If a contractor objects to this contract and insists on using his own standard contract, the committee should view this development with concern and be extremely cautious. They should insist on extensive legal scrutiny of the proposed contract. Any modifications to the AIA contract should also be subject to legal review before the document is signed.

Negotiating and executing the contract with the general contractor should not be done lightly or hastily. If the committee is to err in this process, let it be at the point of being overly cautious and legally judicious.

Build a Good Relationship with the Contractor

The committee should seek from the outset to establish a team feeling with the contractor. When he is brought on board, he joins the team of the architect and the committee. If the contractor is chosen on the basis outlined in this chapter, the relationship should be initiated in a positive way. In some of the early meetings, the committee may want to emphasize mutual commitment. They may want to appeal to the architect and the contractor even as they share their own spirit of unity. They may ask the architect and the contractor to talk about ways they can all work together most effectively as a team.

The committee will want to avoid the posture of antagonist. Avoid communicating the impression that the committee is suspicious of the contractor. Don't allow the "us-you" syndrome to develop. Instead, keep the team emphasis in the forefront.

One of the ways a team relationship is cultivated is by designating a committee representative to work with the architect and the contractor. Other members of the committee must respect this and channel all communication through this representative. One sure way to create division is for each committee member to go on the job site and tell the contractor what the committee expects. That creates a communication nightmare for the contractor. So, agree at the outset that the committee representative is the only person in the church with authority to communicate with the contractor. (If the church retains an architect for construction-phase responsibility, communication to the contractor should be coordinated with the architect. The general conditions in the contract may require that all communication to the contractor be channeled through the architect.)

Another helpful hint: Find ways to affirm the contractor and compliment him for good work. The committee with an eye only for inferior work will never maximize the team relationship. Rather, the committee will be seen only as a faultfinding, negative group. Let the contractor know you expect quality work, recognize and compliment it, and you will develop a much more constructive relationship than with negative complaints.

There will likely be times when the committee representative will have to be confrontational. Sometimes work is done improperly and inadequately and must be torn out and done over. The committee should be reasonable in asking for corrective action when it is needed and rely heavily on the architect for recommendations according to terms of the construction documents. At times, a spirit of negotiation and an attitude of "give and take" will be required to keep the team relationship viable. The committee should see the contractor as a valuable team member without whom it will not be able to secure the desired building. Contractors often develop great pride and appreciation for the buildings they construct. The committee must be constantly alert to ways to link up with this pride, and structure a relationship that is constructive and wholesome.

11

Using Volunteer Construction Crews

One of the exciting developments of the last part of the twentieth century has been the emphasis on volunteers involved in constructing new church buildings. Thousands of laypersons are now investing vacation time, retirement time, and leisure time in this venture. Millions of dollars have been saved in construction costs and hundreds of small churches have been built. In many instances, volunteers have constructed buildings for churches financially unable to build on their own. In other instances, volunteer labor has enabled a church to construct a building without incurring staggering long-term debt. As a result, many new churches have been given significant impetus for a growing and vital ministry in their areas.

That impetus is a marvelous achievement, but it does not tell the whole story. The rest of the story involves the impact on thousands of volunteers who have participated in construction projects. Many of these volunteers have returned to their churches with a new sense of commitment to missions, a new feeling of personal involvement in missions, and a revitalized Christian experience. Others have caught the vision of need in new work areas, relocated to the area where they served on a volunteer crew, and become personally involved in the work of the church there. Once they discovered the tremendous need for workers in the new church, they could not be satisfied until they had invested their lives in the new work.

The development of the volunteer construction emphasis has been promoted by denominational mission boards and men's departments. Churches interested in exploring the possibilities of using volunteer builders should contact these agencies and departments for suggestions and assistance.

Responsibility of a Church Using Volunteers

The church planning to use volunteers should be aware of some basic responsibilities:

1. *Get professional help to design a functional and practical building.*—Well-designed plans are as important for volunteer builders as for professional builders. The proposed building should be designed to meet the program needs and the growth projections of the church. It should be well-situated on the site as a part of a wise master-site plan that has been carefully developed. Significant help in these areas is available through some denominations. Churches are encouraged to contact their denominational offices for early planning assistance.

2. *Develop plans and schedule volunteer crews well in advance.*—Most churches are not aware of the time required for these assignments. They suppose they can complete them within a matter of four or five months.

The wise principle to follow is to complete the basic planning and schedule the volunteer crews at least nine months in advance. (Remember, many volunteers use vacation time for this work, and they must plan months in advance.) If church leaders start in time, they will have little difficulty meeting the advance planning schedule. However, since many church leaders have never been involved in a building project, they have no idea of the time-consuming process required for local approvals, permits, and related matters. They are often shocked to learn of the delays and time requirements for the entire preconstruction process.

3. *Select plans in keeping with the skill level of volunteers.* —Some information should be available relating to the skills of the volunteer crews expected to participate. Designing a building with masonry walls will be a mistake if the crew does not have masons for the project. A building with complex roofing plans is not a good choice for a volunteer crew that has no expertise in this area. Churches should consult with the volunteer crew coor-

dinators to make certain the plans and the skills of the crews are coordinated.

4. *Communicate your financial situation to the project coordinator in the early planning stages.*—Is there any question about whether you have adequate funds to purchase all materials and equipment needed for the project? If so, let him know this. Don't wait until the volunteers arrive to reveal it. In some instances, volunteers can tap some financial resources, but they need to do this early in the planning process. Of course, in most situations the volunteers will not be able to offer any financial assistance.

5. *Be reasonable in requesting building size and capacity.*—Churches using volunteer construction crews are inclined to plan larger buildings than they would construct otherwise. Since they will not have to pay usual labor costs, they see this as an opportunity to build a larger facility. On the surface, that seems like a reasonable response; however, several problems grow out of that response.

a. The church may overbuild and have more space than they can afford to finish. This is especially true if adequate volunteers have not been recruited to complete the entire project. Some buildings have been left half-finished for several years because funds were exhausted. If a certificate of occupancy is required, the certificate may not be issued until the building is finished.

b. The surplus space may increase maintenance and operational costs to the point where they are a burden for the small, struggling church. Under these circumstances the surplus space becomes a liability and, in some instances, an eyesore. A church can give a witness through its buildings and property. A more effective witness can be given with properly designed and well-maintained facilities than with overbuilt and neglected facilities.

c. The extra space constructed may not be what is needed most for church growth, and adapting it to growth space may be difficult or even impossible. One church with thirty in Sunday School and fifty in worship wanted volunteers to build them a worship center for five hundred. The building would have contained only four classrooms. Moreover, the surplus worship space could not be utilized effectively for Sunday School. In developing this design, the pastor of the church was thinking only of future worship facilities, not of space that would support church growth.

In addition to these problems, there is the issue of the best investment of volunteer construction workers. Obviously, there is a limit to resources available from volunteer crews. When these resources are overinvested in one situation, that is certain to result in underinvestment in another situation. Churches should see these issues as a matter of family concern and not ask for more space than they really need for the next growth cycle. (A growth cycle is a period of growth for which the next building should provide adequately. The length of the cycle depends on how fast the church is growing.) This response calls for a disciplined and sensitive Christian conscience that refuses to seek more volunteer help than a church has a right to expect in view of the needs of other mission situations.

The system for delivering volunteer construction services is still in the developmental stage in some denominations. One of the weaknesses is too little centralization of the resources and requests. Progress is being made toward resolving a part of this difficulty. Some denominational groups are beginning to prioritize requests. However, because of church polity in some religious persuasions, centralization of resources has not been achieved. Consequently, some of the greatest needs may go unmet while some moderate needs are oversupplied. The issue is often determined not by need but by who knows whom and what connections they have with resources for volunteer building projects. Of course, this is a problem extending far beyond the powers of the small church seeking volunteer builders. However, if these churches are realistic in their requests, some volunteer construction resources may be freed for other equally important projects.

6. *Secure adequate insurance for the project.*—This includes liability and builder's risk insurance. In addition, the church will be wise to consult an insurance counselor who is familiar with construction issues to make certain adequate coverage is obtained.

7. *Members of the church requesting volunteer help should be*

prepared to pitch in and work side by side with the volunteers as much as possible.—Some members may be unskilled and may be able only to serve as helpers, but that contribution will be important. Imagine how volunteers who have used vacation time and personal money for travel would feel if local members offered no direct help at all. One of the benefits of a volunteer project is the strong ties developed between volunteers and the members of the local congregation.

8. *Consider some plan for follow-up contact with the volunteers.*—They will be interested in progress reports on the work and in the growth and development of the church. Some churches invite all volunteers back for the dedication services. A Christmas card or words of greeting some months after the project is a thoughtful way to say, "Thanks for your investment with us."

What Volunteers Expect from the Church

Every effort should be made in the early discussion stage to clarify what the church seeking volunteer construction help can provide. Some denominational offices can provide covenant forms that ask for appropriate information. What arrangements can be made for lodging? Will volunteers be housed in local homes or in a church building? What plans will be made for meals? Will the local church provide all meals or only a noon meal at the construction site? Will any special provisions need to be made for local transportation? Volunteers expect all these issues to be clearly defined in writing so they can plan accordingly. In addition, they expect the following:

1. *One person from the church should be designated as the local coordinator for the project.*—This person will be the contact person between the church and the volunteers. He is responsible for early planning and preparations. Any additions or deletions to the plans should be coordinated through this contact person. The local coordinator may need to have two other persons who can become directly responsible for assigned areas of work. This kind of coordination will be important for the protection of the church and the volunteers. Confusion and bedlam could result without it.

2. *All permits, approvals, and reviews should be secured well in advance of the scheduled construction date.*—This includes any of the following issues which are involved with this project:

- Zoning and environmental studies
- Traffic and parking reviews
- Fire and building codes
- All permits related to building

The time required for hearings and reviews will vary from one community to another. In some instances, it may take several months. In others, as little as several weeks. One of the problems may be that some review groups meet only once every three months. The church that fails to meet the deadline for one meeting could be caught in a six-month delay. Another problem can be scheduling public hearings. The trend is toward longer and more involved hearing and review processes, and churches need to be prepared for unexpected delays. Nothing should be left to the last minute because too many hitches can develop in the process.

3. *Complete basic site preparation and foundation work before the volunteers arrive.*—This will require such things as rough grading, plumbing supply and drain lines that are below floor level (if a grade floor or slab is used) and those that penetrate foundation walls and the concrete slab (if designed for that building).

4. *Make certain all building materials and equipment have been purchased and are on the site or ready for delivery when needed.*—Materials used on the interior should be protected from damage until ready for installation. Any possibility of a back order for materials can disrupt the entire project. When materials delay a volunteer crew, both the church and the volunteers lose.

5. *Provide security for all materials and equipment delivered to the site.*—Theft of materials from building sites can be a problem. Fence and/or otherwise secure the area during the construction process.

6. *Times of fellowship and diversion away from the construction project are thoughtful provisions.*—Since many of the volunteers are using vacation time, some churches will want to provide

some opportunities for their guests to see and understand the area, especially for those staying longer than one week. In other instances, the volunteers will want to forego all interruptions to the project.

Suggestions for the Volunteers

The volunteer crew coordinator will benefit from an advance trip to the project site. This may reveal site conditions, local issues, and other challenges that need advance attention. The project may run much more smoothly if these issues are known before the volunteers arrive. Some of the issues may even influence recruiting for the volunteer team.

1. *Make certain all members of the volunteer crew are adequately insured.*—Check with your denominational office to see if they have a plan available. One serious injury in transit or at the construction site can create enormous financial problems. Adequate insurance coverage can provide protection for the volunteers and the church.

2. *Be careful not to exert undue influence regarding the building to be constructed.*—The space should be designed to meet the church's need for growth and development rather than the volunteer's need to construct a building. In a few instances, volunteers have imposed a building design on a mission church because the volunteers had the plans and felt comfortable constructing it. There may be instances when volunteers need to refuse to construct a particular building because it is too large, too poorly designed to meet the church's needs, or for some other reason. However, that decision should be made early in the planning process. By the time the volunteers arrive, all questions about the design and the basic plans should have been resolved.

3. *Volunteers should be cautious about suggesting last-minute changes.*—The changes may affect the way the building will function or the program requirements that have been established. They may relate to a local code of which the volunteers are unaware. In one situation, the plans called for roofing with cedar shingles, but the volunteers suggested it would be more economical and faster to use fiberglass shingles. After a hasty decision, fiberglass shingles were installed. Later they discovered

that local codes required roofing with cedar shingles. The church had to remove the fiberglass and install cedar shingles. That costly change could have been avoided if the volunteer coordinator had checked local codes before making the change.

4. *Volunteers should have a qualified building superintendent for the project.*—In most instances, this means bringing the superintendent as a part of the crew. If multiple crews are involved, one superintendent should remain through the entire project. This can avoid significant frustration and loss of time. Even with a superintendent on site, the volunteers should have their own crew superintendent who knows his crew and is able to use them most effectively.

5. *The volunteer superintendent should relate in a wholesome way to local code officials and building inspectors.*—These local officials can be valuable allies in keeping the project on schedule. Every effort should be made to create a cooperative relationship with them. No purpose will be served by complaining and griping about the codes and inspections. No friends will be won by holding these regulations up to ridicule. Especially offensive is the volunteer who presents himself as an authority, tells of all his construction credentials, and calls into question the local enforcement.

6. *Volunteers should respect local customs and church practices.*—This can be critical in some mission situations where some habits are frowned upon by local Christians. The construction team should remember they are there to help strengthen the church as well as to construct a building. Therefore, the volunteers should avoid any behavior that would offend local members.

Volunteer construction projects can be positive experiences for the builders and the churches involved. However, this will not happen by chance. The keys to maximizing the potential are adequate planning, preparation, and communication. Volunteer builders and church leaders should be honest and open with each other. The entire project should be discussed so surprises are kept at a minimum. Every effort should be made to avoid misunderstandings because of inadequate information or misleading expectations.

12

Struggling with the Relocation Issue

The relocation issue is now a critical concern for an increasingly large number of congregations. This is one of the toughest questions with which many churches deal. It strikes fear in the minds of many pastors and church leaders. *Relocation* is a word some churches shun like the plague. Few decisions create as much anxiety and uneasiness in the average congregation.

Yet, with all its negative factors, relocation is claiming the attention of more churches than ever before. How does one explain this? Why would any church leader want to become embroiled in a church relocation struggle? Why are congregations willing to open up this question, invest enormous energies in finding a solution, and spend multimillion dollar amounts on relocation projects? Answers to these questions are found in the following factors:

1. *Relocation has come to be associated with rapid church growth and megachurch development.*—Some churches which have relocated have experienced phenomenal growth, and this has created, in the minds of some, a law of cause and effect. They assume relocation was the cause of growth. Whether it was or not may be open to question. The fact is, many think relocation created the growth. In other instances, megachurches have relocated and experienced rapid growth. Thus, sometimes a significant connection is assumed between relocation and developing a growing church.

In some areas, relocation is almost a fad. It is the "in" thing for a church to do. For example, a church with four acres of property and an average attendance of 125 in Sunday School voted to buy ten acres and relocate. Their reason was that the four-acre site did not give them enough property to grow to the size they wanted to be. They had sufficient property to grow by 400 percent, but rather than face that challenge, they elected to invest their energies in relocation. One can only wonder if that church chose the best mission and stewardship response.

2. *Sociological and demographic changes have thrust churches into situations where relocation has seemed to be the wisest decision.*—Significant deterioration in the community, a high degree of industrialization, and radical swings in demographics have all been factors in the relocation of many churches. When a community becomes a high-crime area and people fear for their safety, relocation becomes attractive to some congregations. Motivating people to faithful church attendance is a real challenge in the best of circumstances, but when these other factors are injected, the task seems almost impossible. Under these circumstances, a decision to relocate is understandable.

3. *Expanded opportunities for church growth and broader ministries have also been a part of the relocation issue for many churches.*—Being in the center of growth can give a church significant advantages. Having sufficient property to launch extensive ministries can also be a great asset. Sometimes these conditions are created by new traffic patterns in the community—the completion of an interstate connector or major thoroughfare. At other times, they are created because the center of residential growth shifts to a completely new area.

4. *A major reason some churches relocate is that they outgrow their sites and no additional property is available for purchase.*—In other instances, property is available but the cost makes it prohibitive for the church. Many churches deal with these limitations for years and hope for some solution short of relocation. Eventually, they face the fact that no solution is available and move ahead with relocation plans.

5. *Some churches are forced to relocate because they have grown to a point beyond the community's capability of accommodating the traffic they generate.*—For example, a growing church in a residential area needs to build a worship center for six thousand people. They own adequate property for the expansion. However, the area is served only by two-lane streets and

these are not adequate to carry the flow of traffic created by six thousand worshipers. Therefore, the church must decide between maintenance and growth. If it stays in its present location, the best it can hope for is to hold its own. If it is to grow, it must move to an area that can accommodate the volume of traffic it will create.

Another church in a similar residential area served only by two-lane streets has been given the distinct understanding that the zoning commission will not approve a worship center that seats more than one thousand. There are times when the relocation issue is forced upon a church because of factors beyond its control.

6. *Relocation for some churches is simply a matter of correcting a serious mistake that was made in the choice of their first location.*—These churches were hidden away on back roads, dead-end streets, and undeveloped properties. They had been seriously limited by their out-of-the-way locations. Finally, their leaders convinced them to find a good location and start over. In some instances, the rate of growth at the new location has surprised even the most optimistic supporters of relocation. In other instances, when the church has kept its same limited vision and approach to "doing" church, relocation has had little effect.

Facing the Relocation Issue

What is the best way for a church to answer the question of relocation? The issue should be approached in a rational, unemotional manner. Therefore, one of the first steps is to appoint a committee to gather information, make an extensive study, and bring a recommendation to the church. The study should pinpoint all the reasons to consider relocation and all the arguments for remaining at the present site. Each of these reasons and arguments should be analyzed and evaluated. Some of them may prove to be unfounded. Others may be compelling. And some, with new information, may be seen in a different light.

The committee will need to be undaunted in its efforts to find answers to all concerns that are raised. Rumors may perpetuate themselves, but committee members must discover the facts. They must go to property owners to see if there is any chance of buying additional property. They must go to local planning and zoning boards to seek "official" rulings on what is allowable and what chances there are of obtaining variances. They must request property saturation studies to determine the maximum number the property will accommodate in single and dual services. (Some denominations offer special assistance to churches with these studies. Check with your denominational office to see what is available.) They must explore every option so that their report can be comprehensive. Some of the studies recommended in chapter 3 will be appropriate to provide background information.

Once the committee has gathered the information, analyzed it, and reached a conclusion, it should take its recommendation to the church leaders. The leaders will then schedule a time for the entire church to receive the information, discuss the recommendation, and prayerfully seek a solution.

Because of the importance of the relocation question, a church should allow two to four weeks for discussion periods on the issue. A series of town-hall-type meetings prior to the time the vote is taken might help in some instances. The people should feel they are being given adequate time to deal thoroughly with the issues involved and receive answers to their questions. There should be an early announcement of the date the church will vote on the issue. That date should be after adequate discussion periods and town-hall-type meetings have been held.

The meetings scheduled should invite free and open discussion. Every effort should be made to encourage questions, the sharing of concerns, and the free flow of information.

The report and recommendation of the committee should be buttressed with charts and graphs to show trends and project future growth in the community and the church. A site-saturation study can establish the number that can be accommodated on the present site. In some instances, the church will already be close to that point. A financial feasibility study can give estimated costs of purchasing adequate property and expanding at the present site. It can also give projected costs of purchasing new property and relocating. The committee should be fully prepared to answer every question with specific information based on studies and surveys. Estimates based on observations or opinions will not be adequate.

Once the vote is taken, the church will need to accept the decision and move ahead with its work. If the decision is to remain at the present location, the leaders should turn to the tasks at hand with renewed vigor and dedication. If the decision is to relocate, the church will need to set up an organization similar to the one recommended in chapter 2.

Four Challenges in Relocation

1. Maintaining the Unity of the Fellowship

The major challenge in the relocation issue is to maintain the unity of the church fellowship as the congregation moves through the process. The basic relocation strategy should be developed with this in mind. No effort should be spared to preserve church unity. Even in the best of circumstances, this will prove to be a monumental assignment. A number of potentially divisive issues will test the fellowship strength of the best of churches. These issues call for the best energies and resources of the most capable church staff.

One of the keys to maintaining church unity is keeping the focus on mission. Rick White, pastor of First Baptist Church, Franklin, Tennessee, says:

> Churches must determine what their mission is going to be before they can legitimately answer the question of relocation. In the case of First Baptist Church, Franklin, we were committed to reaching people. That commitment existed long before the decision to relocate came about. We were, in fact, reaching people in our former location with inadequate facilities. The decision to relocate simply became a better vehicle for the church to carry out its mission.[1]

Another key to maintaining unity is providing full and adequate communication. A 1989 survey of relocated churches indicated communication is essential to a successful project. Respondents to the survey repeatedly pointed to this as a major challenge. Some of the comments were:

"Keep members informed—communicate!"

"We had no division. We kept the people informed with 'town meetings.'"

"The biggest mistake . . . to avoid is a lack of information and communication . . . clear and ongoing communication is needed."[2]

Church leaders should be reminded that communication is a two-way street. It is more than two people talking past each other. Communication involves listening as well as talking. It is not an effort at indoctrination—trying to win someone to your point of view. It is a venture in sharing and understanding. Church members need to feel their leaders are not just talking to them but they are listening: hearing what they have to say, sensing their concerns, and understanding their anxieties.

Still another key to maintaining unity of fellowship is keeping the emphasis on strengthening personal relationships even in the face of differing opinions. The simple fact is not all the members will agree on the relocation question, the purchase of new property, or the plans for the new building. Spiritual maturity may be gauged, in part, by the way we respond to people who disagree with us. Spiritual vitality in a church is indicated by the way members handle divisive issues.

Church leaders should prepare the congregation for relocation discussion by emphasizing the distinction between the point being debated and the person debating. One can oppose and reject an issue without rejecting the person advocating it. Families have to learn to do this to survive. A husband and wife do not build a strong marriage because they agree on everything but because they learn to respect each other and accept their differences. Many church members need help in this area, so leaders should offer specific help and encouragement as the church prepares to deal with relocation.

2. Securing Adequate, Well-located Property

After deciding to relocate, one of the most critical early decisions will be the selection of a new site. The committee charged with this assignment should study chapter 4. It will need to understand the characteristics of a good location and be alert to problems that can be encountered in site selection. It should confer with professionals in the process of site selection.

Denominational personnel and local architects can provide valuable counsel as a committee weighs the pros and cons of various sites. Too often, committees obtain a site and then bring in a professional who immediately sees problems with the selection. Since the property has already been purchased, the church may have to live with the site limitations. Wisdom leads a committee to obtain input and secure the counsel of qualified professionals before a site is purchased. The time and money involved (if any) in obtaining this counsel may be the best investment a church can make at this point. It can prevent serious mistakes, save significant sums of money, and put a church in a location where growth opportunities are not restricted by negative factors.

3. Developing a Sound Financial Plan

Under the best of circumstances, church relocation presents a formidable challenge to the congregation. The first phase of construction on the new site must provide for present basic needs and for space for the next growth cycle. The cost of this construction, plus the cost of the new property, can impose an enormous financial burden on the church. Those dealing with these issues need to carefully study chapter 5. Counsel offered in that chapter can open new doors of opportunity and save churches hundreds of thousands of dollars in financing costs. The most critical single factor in a sound financial plan may be timing. Leaders desperately need to be proactive in helping the church prepare in advance for the financial pressures of relocation.

4. Balancing Worship and Educational Growth Provisions

Many church leaders have learned (though some are a bit slower than others in coming to this awareness) that both worship and educational space provisions are crucial to church growth. Therefore, growth space in both these areas is essential for each phase of development on the new property. Churches concerning themselves with space provisions in only one of these areas often fail to maximize their growth potential. One of the most difficult problems in relocation is deciding which facilities will be provided in the first phase of construction. A sizable number in the congregation will insist that a significant worship center be built first. They think this facility will be the key to growth. Those who understand the importance of a strong Sunday School will insist that adequate space be provided for Sunday School growth. The dilemma is that many churches cannot do what both these groups want to do. The financial demands of the project would be more than they could handle. Therefore, the challenge is to develop the first phase of construction so that the buildings will support a growth strategy for both worship and Sunday School.

This does not mean that the capacity of both facilities must be identical. It simply means that the church must have a workable plan for growth in both worship and Sunday School. Dual services or Sunday Schools may be a part of that plan. For example, one church may decide to build a first unit for 400 in Sunday School and only 300 in worship. Its plan is to have dual worship services to bring worship potential to 550 during its first growth phase. Another church may decide to build for only 300 in Sunday School and 550 in worship. Its plan is to have dual Sunday Schools until it can build a second educational unit. The latter church would face a real problem if it were opposed to dual Sunday Schools and expected to continue to grow even after educational space was saturated. In the average situation, growth would cease when Sunday School space was saturated, unless some provision was made for additional growth space or dual Sunday Schools were started.

Unfortunately, many churches which have relocated have overlooked this challenge in designing their first buildings. They have overbuilt worship space and underbuilt educational space with no intention of starting dual Sunday Schools. As a result, they have grown only to the capacity of their educational space and have never filled the worship space. Lack of Sunday School space may not be the only reason many of these churches have plateaued, but it seems to be a significant factor.

Questions about Relocation

Will Relocation Lead to Growth?

There is nothing in the relocation experience that alone will turn a church around with a sudden burst of growth. A dead church that relocates will still be a dead church unless something happens to breathe spiritual life and vitality into its services and ministry. Growth will come in relocation only if the church develops and implements a sound growth strategy. Growth comes only when churches do those things which produce growth.

These facts were underscored in a 1989 survey by the Research Services Department at the Southern Baptist Sunday School Board. The survey involved 188 churches that had relocated. The survey revealed that 50 percent of the churches experienced more than 20 percent growth in Sunday School attendance the first year after relocating. But 21 percent of the churches had no growth at all during the first year, and some of the churches actually had a decline in attendance after relocating.[3]

The survey was not designed to discover why churches failed to grow after relocating. The assumption is that they were not growing before relocation, and they did nothing after relocating to change that situation. When will we recognize the simple fact that church growth is not a strange and unexplainable phenomenon? It is the direct result of growth actions. Churches grow not by accident but by design. Relocation, within itself, is not a growth action. Opportunities for growth may be greatly increased as a result of wisely planned and carefully executed relocation, but growth occurs only as a direct result of growth actions, activities, and ministries.

What Happens to the Old Property and Buildings?

1. In some instances, the plan is to leave a functioning church at the old location. There are several ways to achieve this:

a. Begin a satellite church involving a continuing relationship with the church that is relocating. There are a number of challenges in this venture. One of the major ones is financial. Most relocating churches need the income from the sale of the old property in order to develop a financial package they can handle. In a satellite relationship, there will usually be an early period when the satellite program must be heavily subsidized by the mother congregation. This comes at a time of such heavy financial demands on the relocating group that they may not be able to continue to fund the satellite.

b. Some of the congregation may decide to remain at the original site and continue a church ministry there. Sometimes a special arrangement is made with this group so they can purchase the property at an attractive cost. Other churches may simply give the property to the group. There are, of course, some thorny problems with each of these alternatives. For example, if part of the membership remains and has to buy the buildings they helped pay for initially, that can create real resentment. On the other hand, giving the property to the group that remains can be a bitter pill for the relocating group which needs funds badly. These issues will require the best of Christian grace and love if they are to be resolved in a way that gives an authentic witness to the community.

The property is sometimes given to the denomination with the stipulation that a mission be started there. In some situations, this can open up significant possibilities for a continuing witness in that community. Churches dealing with this question need to consider not only the financial issues but the larger issues of their Great Commission responsibility.

3. The property may be sold to a smaller sister church or to another denomination. Most churches probably feel better about selling to another church in their denomination. But there is usually little opposition to selling to another evangelical congregation. Many churches would have difficulty selling to a fringe, sect group whose theology was viewed as unchristian.

4. Some churches put their property on the market to sell to any buyer. As a result, the facilities may become an office complex, a retail outlet or a restaurant, or be used for any number of other purposes. The 1989 survey referred to earlier found that about 40 percent of the relocating churches sold their property to nonchurch organizations and 25 percent sold to other churches.[4]

5. Some churches are unable to sell their property; it is unused and allowed to deteriorate, so the buildings eventually become worthless. This probably happens most often in a community that is in a state of rapid decline with low property values.

What Percentage of the Value of the Property Can Be Expected from a Sale?

This will vary depending upon a number of factors. Some valuable properties will bring top prices. One church in Washington state obtained enough from the sale of their property to purchase a new site and pay cash for their new facilities. Unfortunately, that is rare. Many properties of relocating churches have little resale value. In the majority of cases, the church will not receive what they regard as full value for the property. The survey in 1989 found 30 percent of the churches which sold their old property received less than 75 percent of the appraised value.

There are several caution points relocating churches should consider as they anticipate the sale of their old property.[5]

1. Do not base the financial plan for relocation on the assumption of a quick sale. Some churches with contracts on their old property have proceeded with relocation only to have the sale fall through at the last minute. Others have relocated, not been able to sell the old property, and found themselves in a serious financial crisis. A sound approach is to assume there may not be a quick sale and to plan for that eventuality.

2. Be prepared to accept less than the appraised value of the property. In most instances, church property is not in great demand. Any reasonable offer should be given careful consideration. This does not mean a church with good, marketable property should sell with haste. It does mean the church needs an objective evaluation and recommendation from real-estate authorities in the area. Church members may be inclined to overstate the case for value and sales potential. An outside appraisal will give the church a more objective basis for making a decision.

3. If relocation is contingent upon income from the sale of the property, be cautious about beginning new construction until the property is sold. Avoid the kind of haste that will overcommit the church financially if the property does not sell.

How Can a Church Serve Its Previous Field After Relocating?

This question assumes relocation will place the church out of range of its previous field. However, the 1989 survey found that one-third of the churches moved less than two miles, and two thirds of the churches were still within four miles of their previous location.[6] In many instances, churches will be nearer a greater number of their members after relocation than they were before relocating. Under these circumstances, ministry to their previous fields should be no problem. The real challenge may be dealing with the perception that the church has moved away from the old community. Some suggestions for dealing with that perception are:

1. Provide a transportation ministry for those in the previous community so that every person will have convenient access to the new location.
2. Concentrate on maintaining a visible ministry in visitation and pastoral care in the previous community. There is wisdom in systematic pastoral visits and deacon family ministry visits on a more frequent basis in that community for the first year or so after relocation. Plan efforts to communicate that the church is not abandoning the people who reside in the previous area.

What is a Reasonable Timetable to Establish for Relocation?

The time between the relocation decision and the move to the new site will be much longer than most expect. Once the decision to relocate is made, there is often a sense of urgency in implementing it. Generally, there is wisdom in moving to the new location as soon as possible. However, churches need to avoid frantic haste and rushed decision making. Time must be allowed for comprehensive planning and responsible fund-raising. Churches should not become obsessed with a rigid time-table forcing them to "fast track" the relocation project. The work and ministry of the church should not be put on hold while every energy is invested in the process of relocation. Let the church be the church even while committees, designers, and workers are bringing the relocation dream to reality. That really is our calling—to be the people of God, faithfully doing the Father's will. Relocation is not the central issue in our calling. It is only one of many issues the church learns to deal with as it fulfills its calling.

Notes

1. Robert Lowry, "When a Church Relocates, Part 1," *The Quarterly Review*, April, May, June 1990, 49.
2. Ibid., 52-53.
3. Lewis Wingo, "Church Relocation Study," *Baptist Sunday School Board Research Report*, Nashville, March 1989, 23.
4. Ibid., 20.
5. Ibid., 20.
6. Ibid., 13.

APPENDIX A

Functions of the Subcommittees

Chapter 3 gives the basic plan for developing an organization for church building programs. Appendix A deals with the subcommittees and their work assignments. The contents of appendix A are an adaptation and revision of similar material in *Church Property/Building Guidebook* by T. Lee Anderton, published in 1980 by Convention Press.

Organizing the Subcommittees

• The chairperson for each subcommittee is selected by the church and is a member of the building-steering committee.

• The other members of the subcommittee may be elected by the church or may be recruited and enlisted by the chairperson.

• From three to five members are suggested for most subcommittees. If workgroups are used, a good plan is to have one member on the subcommittee for each workgroup that will function within the subcommittee. The chairperson of each workgroup is a member of the subcommittee.

The secretary for each subcommittee is appointed by the chairperson of the subcommittee.

Job Description for Chairperson of Subcommittees

• Serves as a member of the building-steering committee

• Organizes the subcommittee into workgroups as needed

• Schedules meeting dates for the subcommittee and informs secretary to notify members

• Maintains a continuing relationship with the other subcommittees related to work assignments

• Correlates the findings and recommendations of the work-groups
• Keeps the steering committee informed about the work and progress of the subcommittee
• Drafts recommendations of the subcommittee and presents them to the steering committee

Job Description for Secretary of Subcommittee

• Keeps minutes of meetings
• Assists in drafting recommendations
• Prepares and distributes reports
• Informs members of meeting dates and times

The Function and Organization of Workgroups and Subworkgroups

Workgroups and subworkgroups are often used on sizable projects. These groups are selected and given specific assignments for a limited phase of work. Generally, the workgroups are made up of those persons who are already heavily involved in a particular area of work. For example, the music workgroup would be selected from those who are involved in the music program. In some instances, there may be reason to select at least one person for a workgroup who is not personally involved in the particular area being studied. The work of the various groups is closely interrelated and communication should be carefully maintained between them.

Publicity Subcommittee

The responsibility of this subcommittee is to keep the members of the congregation informed about the project. Adequate publicity can stimulate and maintain interest, support, and participation. Informed members will usually be more responsible members. The need for the building and the provisions of the building should be continually kept before the people. The underlying purpose of the building program should be kept in central focus. Nothing about the new building should be taken for granted, for communication requires repetition and reinforcement.

The subcommittee should be composed of members who recognize the importance and value of good publicity. The subcommittee will be strengthened if its members have training and expertise in public relations. They will need to be able to distinguish between news that has general or community appeal and news that is of interest only to the church family. They will use radio, television, and newspapers to tell the story and will employ church papers, direct mail, and visuals such as posters and streamers to focus attention on noteworthy concerns.

Work of the Publicity Subcommittee

• Keep informed about the actions and recommendations of the other subcommittees and the steering committee.

• Discover and utilize as many channels of publicity as possible to promote the project.

• Keep the church informed about developments in the building program and encourage full support of the project.

• Establish and maintain rapport with local news media, keeping in mind media criteria for newsworthy events, programs, and actions. (See app. E for some special promotion possibilities.)

Church Growth Subcommittee

The church that intends to reach and minister to its community will need to discover what the challenges and opportunities are. Need for such information will lead the church to conduct various community studies to locate people who are unchurched and to determine the kinds of programs and facilities needed to reach them.

This group should be composed of persons who have a vision and a concern for church growth. Persons not vitally interested in church growth can hardly be expected to do the kind of work required for this assignment. Members of the group should possess the skills needed to organize and implement serious community studies.

Work of the Church Growth Subcommittee

• Review current resource material on community studies with special attention to securing, classifying, and analyzing commu-

Church Growth Subcommittee

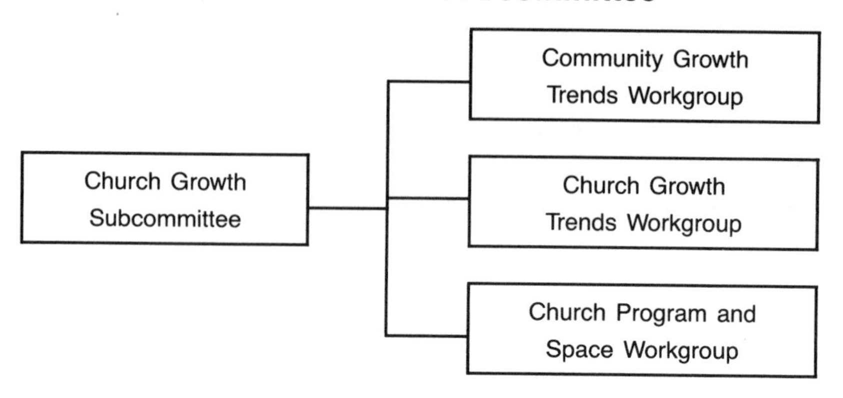

nity information. Study chapter 3 and determine the scope and extent of the community data desired.

• Schedule and conduct the needed surveys and research, including a community religious census.

• Analyze the data and prepare charts, graphs, and maps to visually reinforce the presentation of the data to the steering committee and the church.

• Study church records to determine growth patterns of the past and trends for the future. Try to identify factors that probably influenced the patterns and trends of the past.

• Determine the projections for community growth for the next ten years and evaluate the possibilities for church growth during this period.

• Develop recommendations for programs and ministries that are needed in the community and present them to the steering committee for discussion and approval.

Organizing Workgroups

Because of the scope of the church growth subcommittee assignment, several workgroups are recommended.

1. Community Growth Trends Workgroup

This group can divide its assignment into several subworkgroups such as: housing trends, commercial and industrial trends, population trends, and others that may apply.

Each subworkgroup will focus on the particular area assigned and secure adequate information relating to trends, developments, and projections in that area. They will give special attention to population statistics, economic conditions, trends in land use, and other issues of importance. They should study and analyze the data, process it for presentation to the subcommittee, and draw conclusions and lessons from it for church planning.

The preparation of maps, charts, graphs, and visuals to reinforce and communicate the significance of the data will be helpful.

2. Church Growth Trends Workgroup

This workgroup will compile records on enrollment and attendance for Sunday School, Music Ministry, and other programs or ministries, such as day care. If worship attendance data is available, this will also be included. The records should span the last ten years if long-range trends are to be noted.

Analyze the records, looking for trends in enrollment, attendance, baptisms, and growth. Study the peaks and valleys and compare them with events that may explain them. For example, what relation is there to staff changes and the trends? Is there any relation between church emphases and the trends? For instance, what happened in those years when baptisms were up significantly? The object of the study is to see if there are lessons to be learned and applied to church planning for the future.

Various graphs and other visuals should be prepared to enhance the presentation of the report and recommendations of this workgroup.

3. Church Program and Space Workgroup

The duties of this workgroup are:

- Study program space recommendations in the educational and worship resources of your denomination.
- Study present program space assignments and evaluate the location, size, and adequacy of each.
- Secure from program leaders their requests for space improvement and/or enlargement.

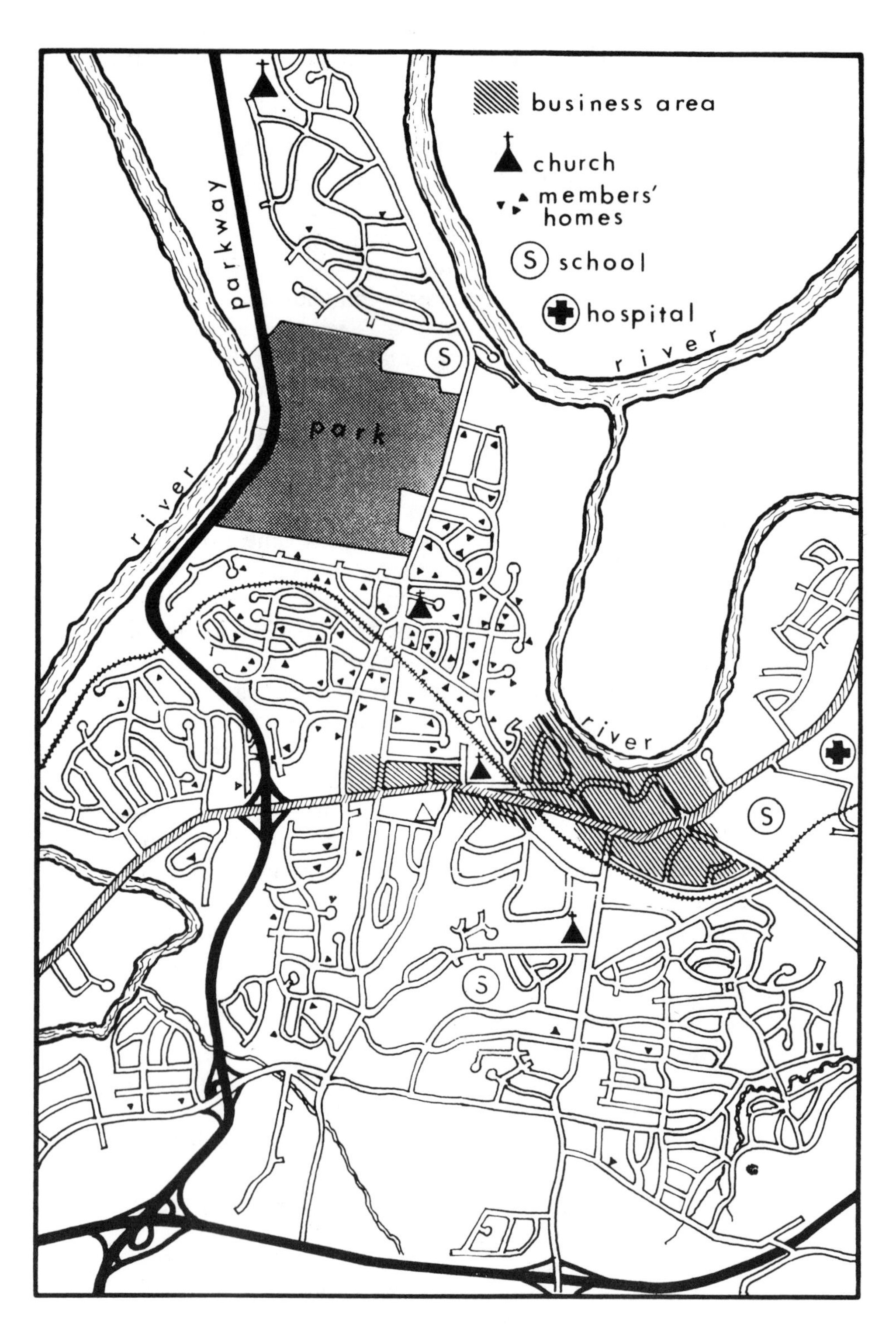

FIGURE 31: CHURCH COMMUNITY MAP

• Study reports and recommendations of the church growth trends workgroup and factor their projections into the study.

• Prepare a written report of observations and recommendations for the church growth subcommittee.

Analyzing Workgroup Reports

When the workgroups complete their work and report to the subcommittee, the latter must interpret, analyze, and compile the information. Their tasks are:

• Project the range of future growth in various church programs, worship services, and related ministries.

• Determine and highlight the factors that will likely affect growth.

• Propose programs and ministries that will be needed if the church is to fulfill its mission.

The subcommittee will prepare a written report of its findings, conclusions, and recommendations and will present it to the building-steering committee. The report may include a map of the community showing pertinent information such as: location of church family residences, neighboring churches, business and industrial areas, and new residential developments. (See fig. 31 for example.)

The subcommittee may want to use a worksheet similar to the one in figure 32 for condensing data in its report.

Church Growth Subcommittee Report

City, town, or community population: Now ________ five years ago ________ 10 years ago ________ 20 years ago ________

Projected population: 5 years ________ 10 years ________

Population of church community (census area): Now ________ 5 years ago ________

Projected population of church community: 5 years ________ 10 years ________

Trend of church community land use is toward: business _____ industrial _____ single-dwelling residential _____ apartment-type residential _____

Number of new homes built: last 12 months ________ projected in 5 years ________ in 10 years ________

Are social or economic changes occurring in the immediate church area? Yes _____ No _____ Describe briefly ______________________________

____

____

Church membership: now ________ 5 years ago ________ projected in 5 years ________ 10 years ________

Worship attendance morning service: now ________ 5 years ago ________ projected in 5 years ________ 10 years ________

Sunday School enrollment: now ________ projected in 5 years ________ in 10 years ________

Is the present property sufficient for projected growth? Yes _____ No _____

Is church site well located in relation to church membership? Yes _____ No _____ Does the church need to move? Yes _____ No _____

Is space in present buildings adequate? Yes _____ No _____

If no, state the needs: ______________________________________

____

____

List below the church's overall needs:

____

____

____
____
____
____

The subcommittee recommends the following priorities: (Use extra sheets as needed.)

1. ____
2. ____
3. ____
4. ____
5. ____
6. ____
7. ____
8. ____

FIGURE 32: CHURCH GROWTH SUBCOMMITTEE REPORT

Property Subcommittee

This subcommittee deals with questions and concerns related to present property and to the purchase of additional property. They will need to understand the characteristics of a good church site and be familiar with the material covered in chapter 4 of this book.

Three persons will be adequate for this subcommittee for most churches. Some churches may want to expand the subcommittee to six or seven members and establish two workgroups: a property needs and evaluation workgroup and a property location and purchasing workgroup.

Work of the Property Subcommittee

This subcommittee will need to maintain close contact with the church growth subcommittee and the church program subcommittee. The findings of the church growth subcommittee will provide essential data for an evaluation of the present site and an indication of whether or not additional property will be needed to

Property Subcommittee

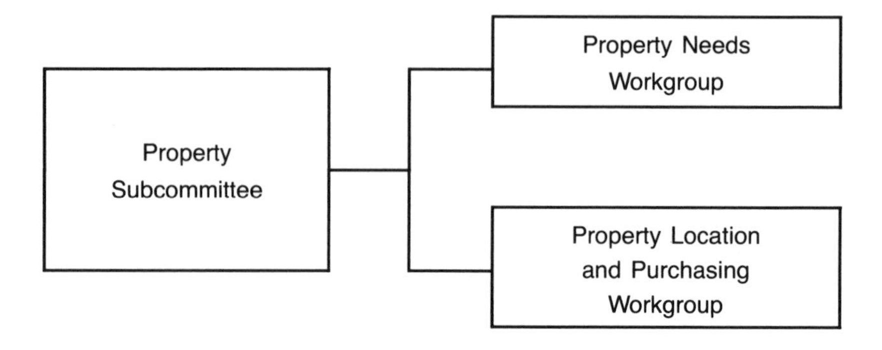

reach the growth potential. The recommendations of the church program subcommittee will also affect the decision as to the amount of property needed. As new programs and ministries are initiated, additional space often will be needed. Therefore, some of the work of the property subcommittee will have to wait until the church growth subcommittee and the church program subcommittee have completed their reports and the steering committee has acted on their recommendations.

Basically, the work of the property subcommittee consists of the following:

• Locate the deed for the property and be certain a qualified surveyor has established the boundaries. Some churches have no idea where their deed is and are only vaguely aware of the location of their boundary lines.

• Discover local code requirements for setback distances, green space, water retention, parking, height restrictions, and environmental impact issues. Determine if there are easements on the property. All these issues will affect the amount of property needed.

• Evaluate the positive and negative factors relating to the present site and determine whether additional property is needed.

• If more property is required, the subcommittee should begin a systematic search to determine what properties adjacent to the church are available and the approximate cost of each.

• At the proper time the subcommittee will make recommendations to the steering committee concerning the location and amount of property proposed for purchase. Members will be available to the steering committee for discussion, evaluation, and additional studies as requested.

• If relocation is an issue, the subcommittee's work will be even more involved. They will need to assist with a complete cost analysis of securing adequate property at a new site and the possibility of selling their present property. The issues of relocating and purchasing a new site require church action. The subcommittee should work through the church's regular channels to purchase property.

Churches that expand the property subcommittee to involve a property needs and evaluation workgroup and a property location and purchasing workgroup will need to divide the work assignments of the subcommittee between these two workgroups. In most instances, the assignments listed above fall naturally into one of these two workgroup areas. However, to avoid confusion, the chairperson of the subcommittee should make specific assignments to the workgroups at the outset.

Program Subcommittee

Wise church building concepts insist that program needs determine design parameters for the building. The program subcommittee must first determine what the church wants to do, and then a building can be designed to provide space support. A church building cannot be designed effectively until there is a clear understanding of church programs and space requirements. The program subcommittee has the basic assignment of developing a comprehensive statement of the programs for which space will be provided and of communicating specific program space needs to the plans subcommittee and the architect. This subcommittee should be responsible for generating a building-program statement that will establish guidelines for the design and construction of the building.

In most churches, this subcommittee will have the largest number of people involved because of the complexity of its assignment. Members of the subcommittee and the workgroups

Program Subcommittee

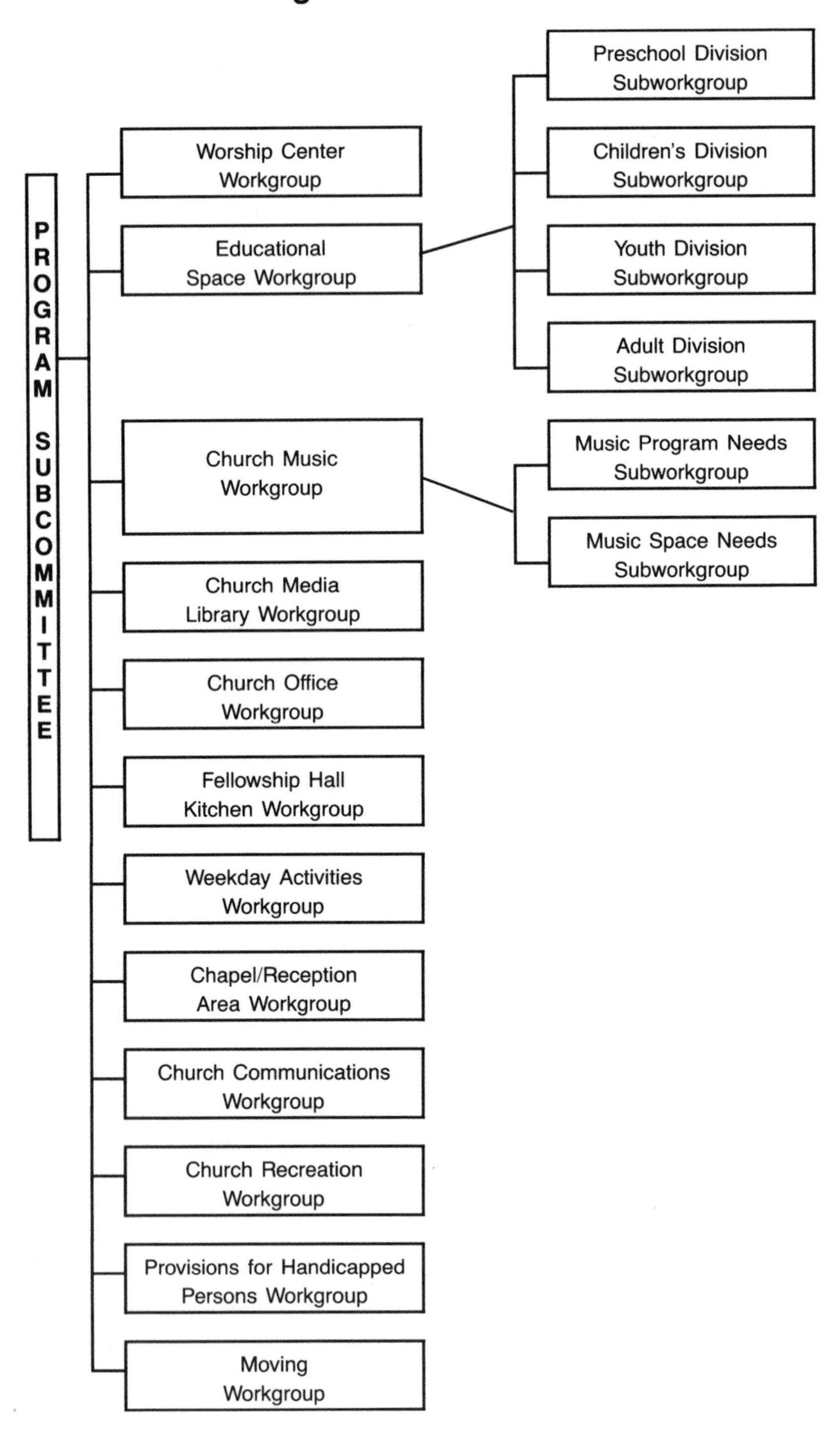

should be persons who are involved in the programs which will be housed in the new building. It is absurd to expect people who have no experience in a program area to develop criteria for that space. Use people who understand the space needs of the programs involved.

Each church should organize its program subcommittee according to the project they anticipate. Small churches may have one person doing the work specified for a workgroup. Medium-size churches and larger churches will have three to five members on workgroups and subworkgroups.

Worship Center Workgroup

This group is responsible for developing a statement concerning the worship space needs of the church. They should study available resources on designing worship centers and familiarize themselves with the subject.

The tasks of the workgroup involve the following:

1. Study the report of the church growth subcommittee and understand the growth challenges that are faced. Pay close attention to the subcommittee's evaluation of existing worship facilities including: physical condition of the building, capacity, and types of services and activities conducted in the worship center.
2. Collaborate with other subcommittees whose task assignments relate to the work of this growth to achieve an underlying coordination.
3. Compile a list of types of services and meetings that may be held in the worship center to see what features need to be provided.
4. Establish the seating capacity desired for the worship center and determine whether or not expandable design features should be included.
5. Confer with Music Ministry program leaders to establish choir capacity, music instrument provision, space for orchestra, handbells, and other performance requirements.
6. Evaluate and determine whether to recommend construction of an interim or a permanent worship facility.
7. Prepare a comprehensive recommendation for the program

subcommittee that will cover all areas of the workgroup's assignment.

Educational Space Workgroup

This group's assignment is to confer with church program leaders and with the church growth subcommittee and project the educational space needed to match growth needs for the next growth cycle. (A growth cycle ranges from three to ten years depending on the rate of growth being experienced.)

The task assignments of this workgroup are:

1. Become familiar with basic resource material on designing educational buildings.
2. Study and evaluate existing educational space with regard to location, room sizes and proportions, and function. As a part of this study, the workgroup may profit from having denominational leaders do an on-site consultation and a space-utilization study.
3. Agree on educational space requirements for each age division based on the resources studied, consultation with church program leaders, and recommended educational space provisions.
4. Determine the educational program needs of the church and how many departments should be provided.
5. Develop growth plans and project capacities needed in each age division for the next growth cycle and for long-range provisions.
6. Secure assistance from the church building-planning department of your denomination.
7. Submit a written report with recommendations to the program subcommittee and be available to explain, interpret, and enlarge upon the report.

Because of the size of the building project, some churches will divide the educational workgroup into the following subworkgroups:

- Preschool division subworkgroup
- Children's division subworkgroup
- Youth division subworkgroup
- Adult division subworkgroup

These groups will make the studies, develop the recommendations, and determine the capacities and provisions to be made for their age groups.

Church Music Workgroup

This group is assigned the responsibility of conferring with church music leaders, developing a statement of music program needs, and defining space requirements that will meet those needs.

The task of this workgroup include the following:

1. Become conversant with recommended music space provisions.
2. Confer with church music leaders to determine the scope of the music program needed by the church and the space requirements for each element of that program.
3. Have direct input with the worship center workgroup, the program subcommittee, and the furnishings subcommittee in determining what musical instruments will be needed. In many situations, the full responsibility for selecting and purchasing these instruments will rest with the music workgroup. However, the educational program workgroup should have a strong voice in determining which departments will have pianos.
4. Prepare a written report with proposals and submit it to the program subcommittee. Be prepared to discuss, defend, and give additional information to assist the subcommittee in its deliberations.

In large building projects, some churches will want to divide the church music workgroup into several subworkgroups, such as:

- Music program subworkgroup
- Music facilities subworkgroup
- Music instruments subworkgroup.

These subworkgroups will be assigned the specific tasks that relate to their area of work.

Church Offices Workgroup

This group determines the administrative space needs of the church. They should confer with the personnel committee to learn if there are plans for adding staff members in the future.

The tasks of the workgroup consist of the following:

1. Confer with all church staff members for recommendations and suggestions about space provisions.
2. Secure and study resource materials about administrative space. Contact your denominational office for suggestions and assistance.
3. Visit other churches and study their administration space.
4. Establish the feasibility of expanding the existing office space, relocating the space to some other area of the existing building, or locating it in the new building. Secure cost estimates for the alternatives, so these may be a part of the final evaluation.
5. Obtain accurate plans of existing office facilities, if there is the possibility that these may be enlarged and expanded.
6. Confer with the church communications subcommittee regarding an interbuilding communications system and other communication issues related to the administrative area.
7. Plan for adequate security for the office staff. In some areas, this will require a buzzer system and electronic door locks.
8. Determine what special space needs will be required for office computer automation and plan accordingly.
9. Consider the importance of locating the administrative area so that it can be enlarged as the church grows.
10. Prepare a written report with recommendations for the subcommittee and be available for discussion and additional input as requested.

Church Media Library Workgroup

This group is responsible for planning adequate facilities for the media library. The media library director and from two to four other members are needed for this workgroup. Those who are selected should be familiar with library services. They should be persons who are willing to study resource materials to determine basic recommendations for space and furnishings.

The task assignments of the church media library workgroup are:

1. Study denominational resources on this subject and become familiar with recommendations and suggestions.

2. Evaluate the present library space and furnishings. If space is inadequate, study the feasibility of expanding the present location, moving to more adequate space in the existing facilities, or locating in a new building.

3. Confer with the church media library committee to determine the extent of the services desired and the space and furnishings needed.

4. Prepare a written report of findings and recommendations for the subcommittee and be available for questions and discussions.

Chapel Workgroup

This group has the responsibility of planning for a chapel, if the church decides to provide one. In some instances, the group may conduct a feasibility study about a chapel.

Three to five persons are adequate for this workgroup. Members should be familiar either with the functions of a chapel or willing to do adequate studies to provide background information for planning and design.

The responsibilities of the group are:

1. Study existing chapel space to determine if it is adequate, or if it can be expanded. If not, plans may be initiated to design a new chapel.

2. Make an adequate study to determine the size chapel needed and the type facility desired.

Fellowship Hall and Kitchen Workgroup

This group is responsible for evaluating existing fellowship hall and kitchen space and making specific recommendations for expanding or providing new facilities as needed.

Three to five members are adequate for this workgroup, in most situations. Some large churches may decide to expand into subworkgroups for specific tasks. For instance, there might be a subworkgroup for the kitchen, another for the fellowship hall, and still another for special provisions for events, such as receptions. The people who serve on these workgroups should be knowledgeable about food service for the size groups projected by the church. They should also have some involvement in planning various fellowship activities for the church.

The following tasks are assigned to this group:

1. Study and evaluate the existing fellowship hall and kitchen with regard to location, capacity, accessibility, and function.
2. Confer with church staff and church fellowship committee to determine the present and projected use of the fellowship hall. Compile information on how it is used, frequency of use, types of food service desired, and the capacity. If there is the perception that a larger facility is needed, how many times a year will the additional space be required? Will that justify the expense involved in constructing new space?
3. Confer with standing church committees such as the fellowship committee and the recreation committee to determine if they have plans that would require expanded space in the fellowship hall.
4. Determine if there are needs for small kitchens to serve other areas of the building.
5. Secure professional help in establishing the desired layout and proper relationship of work space in the kitchen.
6. Evaluate the adequacy of pantry space and storage space for kitchen supplies.
7. If a new fellowship hall is to be constructed, work closely with the plans subcommittee to obtain the best location and layout of the space.
8. If a new or refurbished kitchen is to be provided, determine the equipment needed, secure prices, and place orders at the appropriate time.
9. Prepare a written report with recommendations to the subcommittee and be available for additional input as requested.

Weekday Activities Workgroup

The weekday activities in many churches are sufficient to merit a special planning workgroup's involvement. Some of the ministries involved are: day-care programs for preschool or senior adults, Christian schools, latchkey programs, senior adult ministries, clinics, and community assistance programs. The weekday activities workgroup has the responsibility of evaluating various ministry opportunities and making appropriate recommendations for strengthening, expanding, and/or initiating new ministries.

The workgroup will do the following:

1. Study resource information relating to various ministry opportunities.
2. Conduct surveys to determine the need for weekday ministries. Where there are valid needs and a commitment for church involvement, recommend further studies and research.
3. Once the church has decided to implement a particular ministry, secure information on local and state code requirements for licensing and operation.
4. Confer with other churches who have launched these ministries. Determine what problems, challenges, and growth experiences they have had in these areas.
5. Check with other subcommittees and workgroups to see if they have discovered information which should be considered in planning weekday ministries.
6. Develop specific space provision recommendations for the ministries being planned.
7. Prepare a written report of findings and recommendations to be presented to the subcommittee. Be prepared to respond to requests for additional information or support.

Church Recreation Workgroup

This group has the assignment of determining recreation and social program space needs. Some of these can be met in the church fellowship hall, others can be provided outside, and still others will need space specifically designed for the activities.

Three to five members on this workgroup will be sufficient for most churches. Those planning full recreation buildings will develop a much more comprehensive organization of workgroups and subworkgroups.

This workgroup is assigned the following tasks:

1. Collect resource materials available from your denominational office and from other sources. Study these and become familiar with the opportunities available.
2. Confer with church program leaders to determine their program needs in these areas.
3. Consult with the standing church recreation committee and secure a thorough orientation of their programs and needs. See what they project for future developments in these areas.
4. Explore the scope of the ministry of recreation needed by the church and determine what support provisions exist in the present building program. Those that cannot be provided now may be included in future phases.
5. Submit a written report with findings and recommendations to the program subcommittee and be available for dialogue, if requested.

Church Communications Workgroup

This group has the responsibility of making a careful study of the built-in provisions for a communication system. Included in this study will be: sound-reinforcement systems, intercom and telephones, conduits for closed-circuit television, projectors, built-in projection screens, speakers, hearing-aid systems, provisions for radio and television, and signal systems.

Three to five members are sufficient for this workgroup except in large churches. When large projects are involved several subworkgroups may be needed. In those situations, the following subworkgroups might be appointed:

- Sound-reinforcement system subworkgroup
- Visuals subworkgroup
- Radio and television provisions subworkgroup
- Hearing-aid system subworkgroup
- Built-in communications system subworkgroup

Persons selected for the workgroup and subworkgroups should be knowledgeable about general communication needs for the church. Those who will be dealing with electronic systems should have some familiarity with this area.

Included in the work of this group are the following tasks:

1. Compile detailed information on the present built-in communication system and note any problems and inadequacies.
2. Confer with the worship center, educational, church media library, and fellowship hall and kitchen workgroups to determine needs that relate to their various assignments.
3. Consult with other churches for examples of solutions to communications concerns.
4. Determine what systems and equipment are needed and the costs involved.
5. Determine what special installations are needed in the building, such as conduits, outlets, wiring, projection screens, and window-darkening capabilities.
6. Consult with an acoustical engineer on specifications and installation of sound-reinforcement systems for the worship center.
7. Prepare a written report with findings and recommendations for the subcommittee.
8. After approval by the church and at the proper time, select items to be purchased for installation.

Provisions for Handicapped Persons Workgroup

This group works on adequate provisions for handicapped persons. From three to five members should be appointed. Be certain to include handicapped persons in the group. Others who are selected should be sensitive to the needs of the handicapped and have a commitment to provide full-program accessibility to the church facilities.

This group has the following responsibilities:

1. Study and become familiar with local and state handicapped codes (see ch. 9).
2. Focus the attention of all subcommittees and workgroups on the ideal of program accessibility to all the building. This means that any program offered by the church should be accessible to any person who wants to participate.
3. Develop a written list of all handicapped provisions to be included in the building.

4. Consult with the architect on the design of the building and the estimated cost of incorporating the handicapped provisions.
5. Prepare a written report with full recommendations for the subcommittee.
6. Check the architect's plans in the preliminary and final stages to be certain all requested provisions have been included.

Moving Workgroup

This group is responsible for planning all the logistics involved in moving into the new facility. They do not do the actual moving but develop plans for a smooth transition. Key program leaders in the church should be on this workgroup. The number on the group will be determined by the size of the project. In some situations, subworkgroups will be needed to cover the diverse assignments involved in moving.

The tasks of the group include:

1. Study the plans for the new building to become familiar with the location of all departments and classes.
2. Develop and communicate moving plans well in advance of moving day. These plans will need to be coordinated with department and class leaders so all will know what to expect. In some instances, professional movers may be needed to move most of the furnishings.
3. Confer with the furnishings subcommittee to coordinate the installation of all new furnishings and equipment.
4. Be on hand on moving day to coordinate the process and to give attention to last-minute details.

Finance Subcommittee

The finance subcommittee evaluates the financial potential of the congregation, recommending a fund-raising program, negotiating loans, and setting up a system to pay the construction bills. The number of persons on this subcommittee will range from three to twelve, depending on the size of the project. Persons selected for this assignment should be faithful financial supporters of the church and knowledgeable about financial issues. In most instances, the church finance committee does not serve as the finance subcommittee for a building program.

Finance Subcommittee

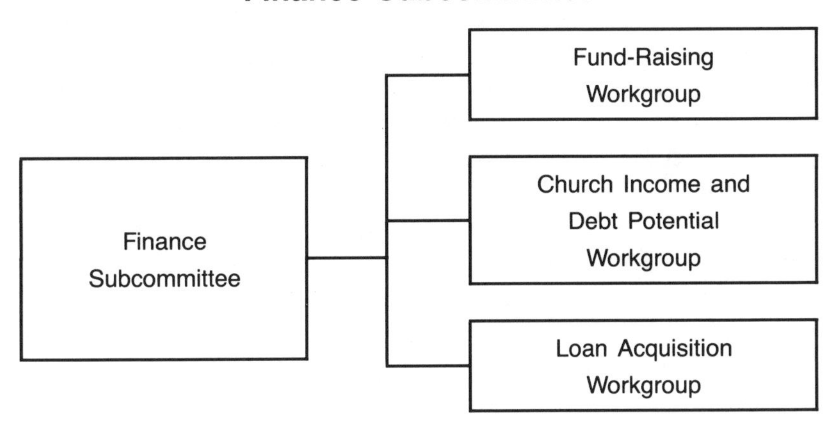

Work of the Finance Subcommittee

This subcommittee has the following tasks:

1. Study chapter 5 in this book and become familiar with principles of sound building financing.
2. Prepare a church financial profile of the past ten years showing budget, income, and designated gifts. Factor inflation into the profile to determine how much real growth has occurred.
3. Check to determine what funds on hand can be used for the new building.
4. Study capital-fund programs and determine which to recommend to the subcommittee. The finance subcommittee for the building project usually does not become the steering committee for the capital-fund effort.
5. Make a comprehensive analysis of the safe debt limit of the church. (See ch. 5 for details.)
6. Study various methods of financing church building programs; investigate sources for long-term financing; and find out what terms are available. Evaluate these programs and terms for the church.
7. Check on church bond companies and the total cost of bond programs. Determine whether there are advantages in using a bond program.
8. Analyze and study requests from other subcommittees,

calculate the total estimated cost of the building project, and determine the amount of money the church will need to borrow.

9. Develop a building budget that includes all costs of the building project. (See sample budget in app. B.)

10. Recommend to the building-steering committee the amount, source, and terms of the construction loan and the long-term loan.

11. Handle all negotiations for the construction loan and the permanent loan.

12. Make timely payments to the architect and contractor as work is completed.

13. Make payments for furnishings and equipment that are not included in the construction contract.

14. Arrange for long-term financing and pay the construction loan at the time of closing.

15. At the conclusion of the project, place all legal documents pertaining to financing in the hands of the church finance committee.

Relationship with Other Subcommittees

The very nature of the finance subcommittee makes a close relationship imperative between it and other subcommittees. Information must be shared, discussed, and evaluated so that the finance subcommittee has a solid basis for decision making. Keeping project costs and financial capabilities in balance will be a real challenge. Payments for completed work will need to be coordinated closely with the construction subcommittee.

Workgroups

Four workgroups will help the entire planning process: fund raising, church income and debt potential, loan acquisition, and building payments. These workgroups have additional responsibilities.

1. Fund-raising Workgroup

The purpose of this group is to conduct studies and recommend a capital-fund program that will enable the church to fund the building project. Help is available through some denominational offices. Check with your denomination to see what is offered. There is wisdom in selecting a separate steering committee for the capital-fund program because special expertise is needed at strategic places on that committee. The fund-raising workgroup simply recommends the capital-fund program and then passes on responsibility to the capital-fund steering committee.

2. Church Income and Debt Potential Workgroup

This group evaluates the financial capabilities of the congregation and determines the parameters for indebtedness. In dealing with their assignment they will need to:

• Study an analysis of the giving patterns in the church and the results of past fund-raising campaigns.

• Check per capita income in the area and estimate the giving potential of the congregation.

• Project church giving for the next five years based on past records and projected growth.

• Develop a financial package that includes cash on hand, income from capital funds, budget allocations, and loan funds. Recommend a proposed package to the finance subcommittee.

3. Loan Acquisition Workgroup

This group checks sources for long-term financing and for negotiating terms and conditions for the funds needed. They will focus on the following:

• A thorough survey of lending institutions to determine possible sources of financing;

• Developing a financial portfolio as outlined in chapter 5. This becomes the basis of a presentation to lending institutions;

• Negotiating and securing both the construction loan and permanent financing.

4. Payments Workgroup

This group has the responsibility of making timely payments for completed work on the building project. They will work with the architect to secure proper certification that the bills received are for work that has been completed.

Their tasks include the following:

• Set up a checking account for the building project and make deposits or draw amounts as needed.
• Establish a procedure for drawing funds on the construction loan as needed.
• Maintain complete records of all funds used in the building program.
• Provide the church with a periodic status report on funds and a final audit at the conclusion of the program.
• Secure evidence of payment from the architect, contractor, subcontractors, and all companies involved in the project. There should be no labor or materials liens on the building. Proper releases to attest to this fact may be required.

Plans Subcommittee

This subcommittee leads the planning process so that the building is designed to meet the program space needs of the church. The size of this subcommittee may range from three to nine. Large churches may need three workgroups: master plan, worship center plan, and educational building plan. Other emphases, such as provisions for the handicapped and energy conservation, can most effectively be coordinated within the subcommittee itself.

Members selected do not need to be "experts" in building plans and construction. Of course, some knowledge in these areas is helpful. But even more important is a spirit of cooperation with the program subcommittee. From the outset, this point should be emphasized: The program drives the building design. The plans subcommittee is charged with the task of overseeing the development of plans that fully support the program statement adopted by the building-steering committee.

The chairperson of the program subcommittee should be assigned as an adviser to the plans subcommittee for continuity between the program-planning process and the space-planning process.

Plans Subcommittee

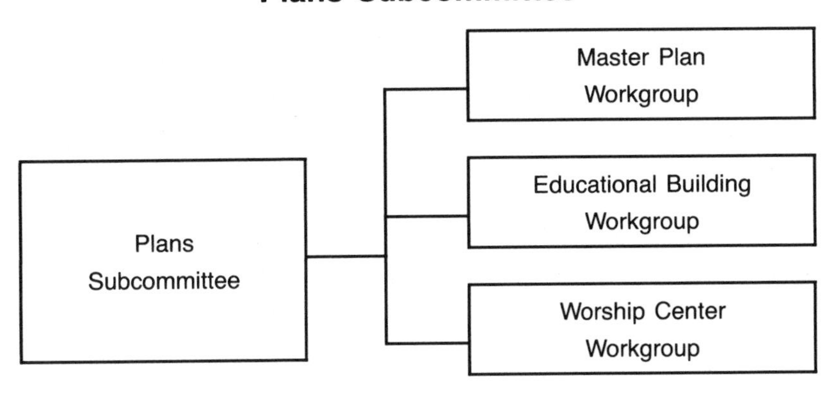

Work of the Plans Subcommittee

Assignments to this subcommittee include:

1. Study chapters 4, 6, 7, 8, and 9 and become informed about space needs for church ministries and programs, master planning, working with the architect, provisions for handicapped persons, and the challenge of developing energy-efficient facilities.

2. Compile information on city, county, and state building codes that will influence the design of the building.

3. Check on the availability of utilities. Do preliminary studies of relative costs of various fuel sources and decide on energy conservation provisions for the new building.

4. Study the recommendations of the program subcommittee and schedule sessions with this group to dialogue about program space needs. The plans subcommittee should be the leading advocate for the provisions recommended by the program subcommittee.

5. Secure assistance from your denominational office in early preliminary planning.

6. Review the preliminary building plans with the program subcommittee and finance subcommittee to correlate projected space needs with the proposed building budget.

7. Work with the architect in the preparation of schematic plans that deal with early design concepts for the project.

8. Review schematic plans with the program subcommittee before making final decisions to accept the plans.

9. Review schematic plans and cost estimates with the finance subcommittee to see if they are in line with the financial parameters that have been developed.

10. Recommend schematic plans to the steering committee so they can share them with the church. Included in this recommendation should be the best cost estimate for the total project. Furnishings and financing should be included in the estimate.

11. Once the schematic plans have been approved by the church, work with the architect in the design development phase. During this period confer with the program subcommittee about any adjustments that may need to be made in space provisions.

12. Present project design plans and revised cost estimates to the steering committee to be recommended to the church. Once the church has approved the plans, changes should be made only for compelling reasons.

13. Work with the architect as he develops construction drawings and specifications for construction of the buildings.

14. When construction drawings are completed, review them with the construction subcommittee, and then turn the plans over to the latter group.

Workgroup Assignments

Churches large enough to develop workgroups for the plans subcommittee should assign these groups tasks as follows:

• Master Plan Workgroup

This group works to secure a comprehensive master-site plan for the property. They will need to deal with the following:

1. Study chapter 4 in this book and focus on the material dealing with developing a master plan.

2. Study the findings of the property subcommittee concerning location and the amount of property.

3. Secure immediate and long-term total projections from the program subcommittee.

4. Obtain local code data relating to setback requirements,

height restrictions, fire codes, parking codes, and environmental impact issues.

5. Work with design professionals to develop the master plan.

• Worship Center Plans Workgroup

This group works closely with the worship center workgroup to see that the plans clearly reflect the findings and recommendations of that workgroup. In a sense, they become the liaison between the worship center workgroup and the plans subcommittee.

• Educational Program Plans Workgroup

This group has the responsibility of emphasizing and interpreting the concepts developed by the educational program workgroup. Every effort is made to see that the final plans reflect clearly the needs delineated in the educational program workgroup's study.

Presentation of the Plans to the Church

The presentation to the church of the plans for the new building is most important. The plans and the presentation must be communicated to the congregation. In most instances, the architect should be used in these presentations. Adequate time should be allotted for full and open discussion. Questions and answers should be encouraged. Remember that some graphics do not communicate to people who are not visually oriented. Therefore, extra efforts should be made through models and other visuals to convey the intended message.

In large and complex projects, there is wisdom in giving the congregation a week or two to deliberate before asking for a formal vote. At all cost, avoid the impression that the proposal is being rushed through the business meeting.

Furnishings Subcommittee

This subcommittee deals with all issues related to furnishings. From three to twelve members may be asked to serve on this subcommittee. They should be persons who are familiar with church programs and the appropriate furnishings. Some churches will want to divide the work of this subcommittee into three or four workgroups: worship center furnishings, educational building furnishings, musical instruments, and memorials.

Furnishings Subcommittee

Furnishings Subcommittee

- Educational Furnishings Workgroup
- Worship Center Furnishings Workgroup
- Music Instruments Workgroup
- Memorials Workgroup

Work of the Furnishings Subcommittee

1. Study available resources on furnishing educational buildings. On the basis of these resources, develop a list of recommended furnishings and specifications for each age group.

2. Confer with church program leaders regarding furnishings needed. Consult the church staff if administrative space is involved.

3. Review the written program proposals from the program subcommittee and the findings of the finance and plans subcommittees. These should give clear information on the furnishings requirements for the program space being planned and directions as to how much money is budgeted for these items.

4. Consult the plans subcommittee and the architect on the choice of furnishings most appropriate for the building. (Note: This applies not to educational furnishings but to furnishings in other areas such as foyers and the worship center.)

5. Investigate the sources for all furnishings needed. Check samples to determine the best quality available within the budget. Do not assume that the least expensive furnishings are the best

buy. Sometimes they cost more in terms of years of service. Choose furnishings that are durable.

6. Secure a minimum of three bids for each item desired. Usually, better prices are available on volume purchases, so keep this in mind when obtaining bids. Be certain the bidding documents spell out clear specifications so bids are on comparable items. Detailed data on furnishings and specifications cannot be obtained at the last minute. These must be developed early so that orders can be placed from three to six months before delivery is expected. If pews and pulpit furnishings are involved, even more lead time will be required.

7. Recommend to the steering committee the sources and prices for all the furnishings.

8. Upon approval of the steering committee, place the order for furnishings with specified dates for delivery.

9. The contract with the furnishings companies should specify that items be delivered, unpacked, cleaned, and placed in the appropriate rooms.

Workgroup Assignments

The groups will need to work with other subcommittees and church program leaders in developing specifications and furnishings lists. In most instances, the recommendations and specifications of these subcommittees and leaders will actually form the basis for the workgroup's assignment.

• Worship Center Furnishings Workgroup

This group has the responsibility of furnishings for the worship center. They will deal with pews (unless furnishings are for an interim worship facility), pulpit furnishings, choir chairs, and furnishings for the lobby. Their specific assignments for study and implementation may be drawn from the list of duties of the furnishings subcommittee.

• Educational Furnishings Workgroup

This group is responsible for selecting and recommending furnishings for educational, fellowship, and recreational buildings. In working through this assignment, they will stay in close touch with the educational workgroup, the recreational workgroup, the program subcommittee, the finance subcommittee, and the plans subcommittee. They will follow the general instructions given above to the furnishings subcommittee regarding evaluating, ordering, and obtaining delivery of furnishings.

• Music Instruments Workgroup

The purpose of this workgroup is to secure information to guide in selecting and recommending music instruments needed. If a pipe organ is to be purchased for the worship center, a special committee is often appointed for this purpose. Members of the music instruments workgroup should have some knowledge and appreciation for quality instruments that will give long years of service.

Their assignment is to:

1. Consult with music leaders and church program leaders for recommendations and to determine which rooms need music instruments. All plans for instruments for educational rooms should be coordinated with the educational workgroup.
2. Confer with the finance subcommittee to determine the budget available for the purchase of instruments.
3. Secure professional counsel as needed for organ specifications and evaluation of other instruments.
4. Investigate sources and costs.
5. Provide the architect with general information about tone chambers and other related matters as needed.
6. Recommend instruments and suppliers to the furnishings subcommittee.
7. After the approval of the steering committee, place orders in line with production and delivery time requirements.

• Memorials Workgroup

In many situations, a responsible group can propose memorials, enlist donors, and prepare appropriate recognition for memorial gifts. If there is no leadership in this area, the results may be a hodgepodge of memorial gifts. Persons may have ideas for memorials that do not fit or that are not in good taste. Therefore, a memorials workgroup is needed for planning and coordination.

This workgroup's assignments are:

1. Study the building plans and determine what equipment, furnishings, and musical instruments could be given as memori-

als. Included might be such items as: stained-glass windows, pews, pulpit furnishings, choir chairs, organ, pianos, lobby furnishings, and numerous other items. In addition to these interior items, memorial gifts may also involve landscaping.

2. Prepare a brochure giving a description and the approximate cost of all proposed memorials.

3. Communicate to the congregation the many opportunities to give memorial gifts.

4. Work with the plans subcommittee to design an area of the church where appropriate recognition can be given to all memorial gift donors.

Construction Subcommittee

This subcommittee works with design professionals and the building trades in the actual process of construction. The specific duties of the subcommittee will depend on the delivery system selected for construction. Three to five members are adequate for this subcommittee. There are good reasons for keeping the size small. Direct communication and coordination between this subcommittee and the architect and contractor is essential. The lines of communication must be clear and uncomplicated; therefore, workgroups are not recommended for this assignment. The members of this subcommittee should have some knowledge of the construction process, but they need not be "experts" in this field. The work of this subcommittee will be greatly expanded if the church serves as its own contractor or uses one of the other delivery systems that places much of the general contractor's responsibility on the church.

Work of the Construction Subcommittee

1. Study chapters 6 and 10 and become familiar with the relationships and responsibilities involved in the construction process.

2. Study the construction documents for the proposed building and become familiar with them.

3. Consult the architect and be prepared to determine the type contract to be used for the construction.

4. Work with the architect in securing bids, negotiating with the

contractor, getting church approval of the contractor and subcontractors, and contracting for the work to be done.

5. Consult with the church's regular legal counsel in drawing up and signing contracts for the project.

6. Work with the architect to see that proper building permits are secured.

7. Designate the chairperson of the subcommittee or one member to be the contact person with the architect and the contractor. Emphasize that all instructions and agreements are to be channeled through this person.

8. Work closely with the plans subcommittee to see that the intent of the plans and the program provisions are not changed.

9. Maintain appropriate financial records for the project. If there is no firm contract price, a cost-control budget should be maintained. This should show expenditures to date and projected final costs. Without appropriate cost control, the project can easily get out of hand and end up considerably over budget.

10. Consult with the architect in handling all change orders during construction.

11. After certification by the architect that the specified work has been completed, approve payments to the contractor and refer to the finance committee.

12. Serve as a clearinghouse for all subcommittees having responsibilities of selecting materials, color, furnishings, and equipment.

13. Select and approve items in the contract for which allowances have been made.

14. Clear all major items with the steering committee before approving or rejecting them.

15. Report regularly to the steering committee on the progress of the construction. Furnish information and reports that can be used by the publicity subcommittee.

16. Accompany the architect on periodic inspections of the building while it is under construction and consult with him on any problems encountered.

17. Cooperate with the architect and the finance committee in making payments due during construction and at the completion of the building.

18. Work with the architect in the final inspection process. The architect is responsible for making an inspection of the building when the contractor says it is finished. During the inspection he develops a punch-list of items not acceptable. After the contractor has corrected items on the punch-list, the architect and the subcommittee chairperson (or full subcommittee) will inspect the building. If there are problems, a new punch-list is made, and the contractor corrects these before preparing a final certificate of completion. Usually, a one-year warranty is given to protect the church. During that year the contractor is responsible to correct all faulty workmanship.

19. Secure from the architect one set of plans and specifications that show all changes made during construction and the location of supply and waste lines. These documents will be valuable in future years when maintenance problems occur and when renovations or additions are made.

APPENDIX B

Financial Helps

Building Budget Worksheet

	Cost	Totals
Additional Property		________
Construction Costs		
Excavation, grading, site preparation	________	
Paving and sidewalks	________	
Building	________	
Utility service	________	
Other	________	
Subtotal		________
Construction Contingency (construction cost × 5%)		________
Fees		
Design Fees (Architect, Engineers, etc.)	________	
Special Consultant Fees	________	
City Impact Fees	________	
Geotechnical Engineering	________	
Construction Testing	________	
Government Permits, Fees	________	
Subtotal		________
Miscellaneous		
Landscaping	________	
Furnishings	________	
Insurance	________	
Performance Bond	________	
Other Miscellaneous	________	
Subtotal		________

Finance Costs		
Construction Financing	________	
Loan Initiation Fees	________	
Closing Costs for Loan	________	
Subtotal		________
Total Projected Costs		________

Note: Study chapter 5 as the building budget is being developed. Remember in the early planning that many of the costs are simply estimates that may have to be adjusted when more complete data is available.

Examples of Financial Packaging

Following are five ways a church might package its financial plans to provide for a new building. The constant factors in each plan are annual income and construction costs. The variables are such factors as cash-on-hand, fund raising, and long-term financing. The five packages are intended to illustrate ways churches can be creative in financing and save significant costs.

	Plan A
Annual Income	$182,000
Building Fund	$50,000
Building Budget	$500,000

Plans:

- Conduct a capital-fund program immediately
- Begin construction eighteen months later
- Complete construction nine months before three-year capital-fund program ends

Financial Worksheet:

Building fund plus two-year's interest	$ 57,245
Capital funds pledged	$309,400
Available twenty-seven months later	$238,569
Total available at closing	$295,814
Minus Construction financing	$ 10,000
Amount to be financed	$215,000

If monthly loan payments of $3,304 plus capital-fund gifts of $8,594 are paid for the first nine months, the loan balance can be reduced to $120,947 at that time. The church could then retire the loan in four years.

Interest paid on loan $39,339
Interest on construction loan $10,000
Total interest... $49,339

Building debt paid 4.75 years after building completed.

Plan B

Annual Income............ $182,000
Building Fund 0
Building Budget $500,000

Plans:
- Conduct a capital-fund program immediately
- Begin construction at same time capital-fund gifts start
- Complete construction twenty-seven months before capital-fund program ends

Financial Worksheet:
Capital funds pledged $309,400
Available nine months later .... $ 77,348
Total available at closing.............................. $ 77,348
Minus construction financing.............................. $ 25,000
Amount to be financed....................................... $447,652

If monthly payments of $5,109 plus capital fund gifts of $8,594 are paid for the first twenty-seven months, the loan balance will be reduced to $155,055. That balance could then be repaid in three more years with monthly payments of $5,109.

Interest paid on loan $105,111
Construction loan interest .... $ 25,000
Total interest.. $130,111

Building debt paid 5.25 years after building completed.

Plan C
(Church Bond Plan)

Annual Income $182,000
Building Fund 0
Building Budget $500,000

Plans:

- Raise $50,000 in cash within nine months
- Conduct a bond program immediately
- Begin construction three months later
- Complete construction one year after beginning bond program

Financial Worksheet:

Cash available at closing .... $ 50,000
Income from bonds sold..................................... $450,000

The $450,000 bond issue was sold at 10 percent interest. Other costs of the bond issue bring total cost to the church to 11 percent. To amortize this over fifteen years will require monthly payments of $5,116.

Interest paid over the fifteen years: $470,970

Plan D

(A Type of Pay as You Go Plan)

Annual Income	$182,000
Building Fund	0
Building Budget	$500,000

Plans:

- Conduct a capital-fund program immediately
- Begin making monthly deposits from budget to a building fund
- Delay construction for twenty-seven months so construction is completed as capital-fund program ends

Financial Worksheet:

Capital funds pledged $309,400
Full amount plus interest
available three years later............................. $347,709
Funds from budget allocation:
1st year $2,000 a month plus interest............... $ 28,888
2nd year $2,500 a month plus interest .... $ 33,591
3rd year $3,000 a month plus interest............. $ 37,496
Total available at conclusion
of capital-fund program $447,684

Minus construction financing.................................$ 1,046
Total available $446,638

If construction loan of $53,362 is extended for six months, the following provisions might be made:

Ask members to extend capital-fund pledges
for four months $33,976
Make monthly payments from budget of $4,153
for five months $20,765
This will repay the construction loan in five months.

Total interest paid: $2,425

Plan E

(Completely Financed by Capital Funds)

Annual Income	$182,000
Building Fund	0
Building Budget	$500,000

Plans:

- Conduct a capital-fund program immediately
- Begin construction three months later
- Complete construction as first year of capital funding is completed

Financial Worksheet:

Capital funds pledged $309,400
Available one year later...................................$105,000
Minus construction financing...............................$ 30,000
Total available at closing..................................$ 75,000

A loan of $425,000 is negotiated at 11 percent monthly payments of $8,089 will be paid over the next two years using the income from capital funds. This will reduce the loan balance to $312,944. A second capital-fund program will be conducted with a goal of raising $369,000. Monthly payments of $10,245 will be made with capital funds. This will amortize the remaining debt in three years. (Note the monthly payments of $8,089 are only 94 percent of total pledged. Loan payments should not be set at 100 percent of pledged amount if only capital funds are used for payments.)

Interest on loan:	$138,031
Construction financing:	$30,000
Total interest:	$168,031

Building indebtedness paid six years after completion.

Comparison of Five Plans

Plan	*Building Occupied*	*Interest Paid*
A	27 months later	$ 53,405
B	12 months later	$130,111
C	9 months later	$470,970
D	36 months later	$ 2,425
E	12 months later	$168,031

Cost of Timing

Plan C constructed the building twenty-seven months before plan D, but extra interest was $17,354 per month for this twenty-seven-month period ($468,545 extra interest divided by twenty-seven months).

Plan B constructed the building fifteen months before plan A, but extra interest was $5,114 per month for this fifteen-month period ($76,706 extra interest divided by fifteen-months).

There is a strong correlation between timing, capital funding, and the total amount paid in interest.

Notes

1. No closing costs have been factored into this study.
2. No allowance has been made for inflation. In times of high inflation, increased building costs can wipe out compound interest gains.
3. Construction financing costs have been estimated. They will vary from one project to another and cannot be determined with precision until other factors are known.
4. In each plan, the assumption has been made that the total

amount pledged in capital funding actually was received. Many times this will not occur, and the church will have to make up the difference, if the schedules set forth here are to be realized.

APPENDIX C

Steps in a Building Program

I. Survey Phase

A. Identify property and building inadequacies
   1. List general inadequacies
   2. Review list with key program leaders
B. Secure outside help
   1. Request help from your denominational office
   2. Study chapters 2, 3, and appendix A for help in organizing a committee and conducting a building program
C. Secure church action to appoint a building-steering committee
   1. Report property and building inadequacies to the church
   2. Structure the building-steering committee to begin a study directed to the church taking actions to meet property and building needs
D. Organize and train the committee
   1. Appoint subcommittees and workgroups
   2. Train the committee using this book as a guide
E. Explore community needs to discover church opportunities
   1. Survey the community or area served
   2. Determine the specific needs of the people in the community
   3. Brainstorm church's mission
   4. Determine the number of persons who might be reached in each program
F. Develop a comprehensive building program
   1. Define and prepare a written statement of programs to be provided by the church
   2. Determine the number of people for which space will be provided in each church program

G. Evaluate the adequacy and suitability of the church site
   1. Evaluate present location
   2. Determine amount of property needed
H. Prepare a financial plan
   1. Review past and present financial performance
   2. Make initial contact with your denominational office for sources of fund-raising help
   3. Project the amount of money to be raised in an intensive capital-fund campaign
   4. Investigate sources for borrowing funds and potential amounts available
   5. Secure tentative loan commitment from selected loan mortgagee
   6. Determine the maximum funds available for the building program

II. Planning Phase

A. Prepare property use plot and floor plans
   1. Obtain accurate floor plans of existing building
   2. Identify uses of present space and any temporary spaces being used
   3. Examine the structural condition of the church building(s) to determine any repair and/or renovation needs
   4. Determine the amount and type of new space needed
   5. Acquire an accurate plot plan of the church's property including any to be acquired
   6. Secure assistance from denominational office in floor plan studies for a purposed building. If your denomination does not offer this service, secure the services of an architect.
B. Report to the church and secure a church decision on the proposed project
   1. Report findings and recommendations to the church
      a. Identify program needs for which space will be provided
      b. Identify the proposed site development plans and floor plans for immediate space to be constructed

   c. Report the anticipated cost of the immediate building project
   d. Identify the probable means and source of financing the building project
   e. Suggest the growth and other results anticipated from the building project
2. Secure church action on:
   a. The type and amount of space to be constructed
   b. The acquisition of any needed property
   c. The employment of an architect and commitment to working drawings
   d. The plan for financing the project

C. Secure preliminary and design drawings for the project and begin fund-raising campaign
1. Instruct architect to prepare floor plans and cost estimates based on church's approval of type and amount of space to be constructed
2. Begin the fund-raising campaign
3. Present plans and cost estimate to the church for approval
4. Instruct architect to prepare design development plans, including materials and finishes, and prepare revised cost estimates
5. Review drawings and present the plans and cost estimate to the church for approval

III. Construction Phase

A. Secure construction drawings
1. Instruct the architect to prepare construction drawings in line with church-approved design development plans
2. Give the church a progress report when the plans are completed and approved by the steering committee
3. Note: Some of the actions of items II, C and III, A are subject to repetition if the committee and/or the church is not satisfied with the architect's work

B. Begin organizational enlargement and leadership training simultaneously with the start of construction
1. Enlist new workers for an enlarged organization

2. Begin an aggressive and intensive training program for present and new workers
3. Design a "saturation" visitation program to start immediately prior to the occupancy of the new building

C. Select contractor, award contract, and complete building construction
1. With architect's guidance, select contractors from whom bids will be received
2. Furnish contractors with plans for the project, including a list of any alternates, and specify date bids are due
3. Receive bids, open, and review with architect
4. Arrange for permanent financing and secure the construction loan
5. Award contract to selected contractor(s), and notify other contractors of the rejection of their bids
6. Secure bonding and workmen's compensation insurance
7. Order furnishings needed
8. Inspect project periodically with the architect and authorize payments to contractor at appropriate times
9. Make final inspection
10. Approve and accept work after contractor has completed all work according to contract agreements and plan specifications
11. Make final payment to contractor and architect

D. Complete financing arrangements for the building project
1. Make final arrangement with loan company for permanent financing
2. Set up budget amount needed to make loan payments
3. Secure appropriate insurance on the new building

E. Furnish and occupy the new building
1. Inspect new furnishings on delivery
2. Install furnishings after the new building is completed and heating and cooling is functioning
3. Plan to enter the new building with a high attendance and an expanded organization functioning at top efficiency
4. Plan a service of dedication at an appropriate time

Rules of Thumb

Space and Dimension Recommendations

A rule of thumb is useful only in making approximations and should not be used dogmatically. Understanding the variables affecting their values is essential in their application to specific situations. Rules of thumb are used primarily for estimation of property, building space, and other needs prerequisite to actual planning.

Site Planning

- Worship center, educational building, parking:
  One acre per 100-125 attendance
- Recreation building and/or outdoor recreation:
  Two to four additional acres
- Pastor's home not recommended on church site

Worship Center Ground Coverage

- Capacity up to 300: 15-17 square feet per person
- 300-500 capacity: 12-18 square feet per person
- 500 up capacity: 10-18 square feet per person with balconies included

Note: Rectangular buildings with straight row seating require less space per person than buildings with seating that wraps around the platform. In some instances, ten square feet per person is adequate in straight-row seating for buildings with capacity over five hundred.

Educational Building Ground Coverage

- First unit buildings, multiple use:
  30 to 40 square feet per person
- Small buildings: 45 square feet per person
- Larger churches with extensive programs:
  55 square feet per person

Church Recreation Building Ground Coverage

- Gymnasium with only rest rooms/dressing rooms and junior high-size court
  (42 feet × 74 feet) : 6,600 square feet

- Gymnasium, with activities rooms, multipurpose rooms, secondary fellowship function, kitchen, rest rooms, dressing rooms, exercise rooms, running track, etc., senior high-size court (50 feet × 84 feet) : 10,000 to 16,000 square feet

Parking

Statistics assume efficient layout with parking on both sides of drives.

- One space for every 2.5 seats in worship center
- 110-125 spaces per acre when used for parking only
- Parking ground coverage per space:
  Standard:
  90 degree—279 square feet (two-way drive)
  45 degree—290 square feet (one-way drive)
  Compact:
  90 degree—238 square feet (two-way drive)
  45 degree—252 square feet (one-way drive)
- Parking space dimensions:
  Standard, 9 feet by 18 feet
  Compact, 8.5 feet by 16 feet
  Handicapped, 14 feet by 18 feet for single space

Worship Center

Pulpit Platform

- Front to back depth: 7 feet minimum
  larger buildings require 10 feet or more
- Height: 2 feet maximum, less than eleven rows of congregational seating
  3 feet maximum, up to eighteen rows of congregational seating
- Distance platform to front pew:
  7.5 feet minimum
  8.5 feet recommended
  10 to 12 feet with 4 feet for Lord's Supper table platform

Choir Area

- Choir capacity:
  10-12 percent of congregational capacity

- Choir rows:
  3 feet minimum depth
  Back and front rows: 3 feet, 2 inches minimum depth
- Seating:
  Movable chairs at 24″ width per person
- Floor covering:
  Hard surface such as hardwood, stone, or vinyl
  Carpet not recommended under piano or in choir area
- Surfaces:
  Accoustically reflective floor, walls, and ceiling surfaces recommended

Baptistry

- Inside pool dimensions: 4 feet by 6 feet minimum
  4 feet by 7 feet 3½ inches maximum
- Exterior pool dimensions, steps both ends:
  4 feet 6 inches by 12 feet 9 inches minimum,
  4 feet 9 inches by 14 feet maximum
- Water depth: Between 3 feet and 3 feet 6 inches
- Baptistry floor, eighteen inches above last choir row; minimum, 6 inches; maximum, three feet

Congregational Seating

Local building codes and the National Life Safety Code adopted by the locality should be consulted for minimum requirements.

- Row spacing:
  36 inches or more recommended, 34 inches minimum
  48 inches minimum if last row against a wall
- Pew lengths and seating:
  Average space per person, 20 inches width
  13 or 14 persons maximum on each row
  Row length, 21 feet, 6 inches to 23 feet, 4 inches
- Aisle widths (check local codes)
  —Center or main aisle, 4 feet minimum;
  5 feet or more recommended
  —Side aisles, 2 feet, 6 inches minimum;
  Some codes, 3 feet, 8 inches

Vestibule/Lobby

- Worship center entry:
  —1½ to 2½ square feet per seat in worship center
  —Fellowship lobby between education and worship: 15 to 25 percent of the worship center area

Balcony

- Capacity:
  Less than 50 percent of main floor seating
- Riser depth: 3 feet 6 inches for first row
  3 feet 2 inches for the back row
  3 feet for other risers
- Aisles: 4 feet minimum across balcony
- Other aisles: Same as aisle width on main floor
- Stairwells: Two to outside exits
- Balcony location:
  45 feet minimum, platform to balcony
  35 feet minimum, between side balconies
- Sight line: Clear sight line from rear balcony rows to main floor Lord's Supper table and decision areas

Chapel

- Seating capacity:
  50 to 175 at 15 square feet per person
- Brides's dressing room: 12 feet by 12 feet recommended
  8 feet by 10 feet minimum

Steeple Height:

Equal to distance between roof ridge and ground level

Educational Building

Refer to your denominational educational books.

Administrative

- Pastor's study: 250 to 325 square feet recommended
  140 square feet minimum

- Staff offices: 150 to 200 square feet recommended
  120 square feet minimum
- Other office space: Offices for support staff, workroom(s), reception area, storage, rest rooms, lounge, kitchenette, based on church needs

Music

- Rehearsal room: 15 to 20 square feet per person
  Capacity at least 10 percent more than worship center choir area
- Robing rooms: 4 to 6 square feet per person
- Music library: 1 to 2 square feet per choir member
- Orchestral rehearsal room: 25 square feet per person
- Handbell rehearsal room: 20 feet by 30 foot desirable; (Allows for a five-octave set of handbells with twelve ringers, 32 feet of tables)
- Individual practice rooms: 10 to 15 persons at 10 square feet per person
- Voice and piano practice rooms: 8 feet by 10 feet minimum

Media Library

- Size: 2 square feet per person provided for in educational building is recommended; minimum of 1 sq. ft. per person

Fellowship Hall

- Dining capacity: 1/3 to 1/2 educational building capacity recommended
- Space required for table seating:
  12 sq. ft. per person recommended
  10 sq. ft. per person, minimum
  15 sq. ft. for round tables
  Table and chair arrangement determines actual capacity
- Stage requires additional space
- Institutional kitchen: 1/3 to 1/4 size of dining area

Rest rooms

Minimum Number of Fixtures in Rest Rooms

Building Capacity	Women		Men			Preschool	
	WC	L	WC	U	L	WC	L
Diaper Unit							
Up to 100*	2	1	1	1	1	*	
101-200	3	1	2	1	1	1	
201-300	4	2	2	2	2	1	1
301-400	5	2	3	2	2	1	1
401-650	7	3	4	3	3	2	1
651-900	10	4	5	5	4	2	1
901-1200	12	4	6	6	4	3	1

*Increase to 125 if preschool toilets provided.

Church Recreation Building

- Basketball Court:
  - Clear ceiling height, 20 feet minimum, 25 feet desirable
  - Side and end lanes, 3 feet minimum, 10 feet preferred
- Senior high size court: 50 feet by 84 feet
  - Room size: 70 feet by 104 feet preferred
  - (7,280 square feet) plus 3 feet for each additional row of spectator seating
- Junior high size court: 42 feet by 74 feet
  - Room size: 62 feet by 94 feet preferred
    (5,828 square feet) plus 3 feet for each additional row of spectator seating
- Handball/racquetball courts:
  - 20 feet by 40 feet each, 20 feet ceiling height
- Game rooms: 24 feet by 30 feet to 40 feet by 60 feet or more
- Group meeting rooms: 15 square feet per person
- Storage: A direct access room with double-wide doors for roll-in table/chair carts.
  - —Separate storage space for recreational equipment, crafts supplies, kitchen pantry, janitorial supplies, and equipment

- Additional rooms or space:
  Snacks/vending, crafts, exercise, control, office, bowling lanes
- Rest rooms:
  —Rest rooms for gymnasium area, in addition to minimum number in preceding chart
  —Showers, if desired with dressing space and lockers
  —Other provisions such as sauna, steam room, whirlpool may be included

Mechanical Equipment Rooms

- Space requirements:
  —Varies with region/equipment types;
  —Buildings up to 7,000 square feet: 1½ percent of total building space
  —Above 7,000 square feet: 2 percent of building space

Provisions for Handicapped Persons

See chapter 9 for detailed information. Requirements vary and many state codes are based on standards developed by the American National Standards Institute (A.N.S.I.) or the North Carolina building code.

Considerations include:

- Extra wide parking spaces: 10′ space plus 4-foot clearance for wheelchair access
- Building entry: No steps; ramp if steps
- Slope of walks not more than 1 foot in 20 feet
- Slope of ramps not more than 1 inch in 12 inches
- Clearances: 36 inches minimum door width
  —5 feet minimum hallway width for two wheelchairs to pass
  —5 feet, 6 inches minimum hallway width for two persons passing on crutches
  —Rest room dimensions to allow turning radius for wheelchair
- Handrails at ramps; grab bars in toilets
- Wheelchair spaces in the worship center
- Elevators

Financing

Maximum Debt: (total building debt excluding parsonage—2 to 2½ times annual income of previous year
—Recommend no more than 25 to 30 percent of annual income go to debt retirement

Building Project Budget

Percent of Construction Cost

Architect and other fees	6 to 12 percent
Furnishings	8 to 15 percent
Landscape	5 to 15 percent
Contingency	5 percent
Construction loan financing	8 to 10 percent
Financing closing costs	2 to 7 percent

Construction costs will usually be only 70 to 80 percent of total building budget

Capital Fund-Raising

Average fund-raising results:

- One to three times (on occasions more) previous year's budget income for building program and/or debt retirement
- Receipts of 90 to 105 percent of amount pledged over a three-year period
- Results depend on commitment to project, the quality of the church's fellowship, the church's giving potential, and the need for the project

APPENDIX D

Interview Questions for Architects

I. Preinterview

A. Set date, invite architect, and schedule time.
B. Provide the architect with following information:
   1. Site information
   2. Preliminary sketches of project if any are available
   3. General building budget information
   4. Building program information and requirements

(The following information may be reproduced and sent to the architect prior to the interview.)

II. Interview

A. The architect/firm
   1. Give a brief overview of the firm.
      a. Your qualifications and experience.
      b. Have you done other church projects? Describe project.
      c. What is the range of project sizes and costs with which your firm usually works?
      d. May we have a list of previous clients with similar projects?
   2. Describe the services of your firm as they relate to each phase of the architectural and construction process for our project.
   3. Tell us about your firm's associates and technical specialists.
      a. Who in the firm would be primarily responsible for our project?
      b. What other personnel in the firm would be assigned to our project?

c. Would an interview with any of these persons be beneficial?
d. Do you have "in-house" engineering or do you use consulting firms?
e. Are there other specialists who would be needed on our projects?

4. Describe briefly the interrelated roles of the church, architect, and contractor.
5. Based on your perception of our project, how would you propose to work with us?
6. Why do you feel you are the architect/firm who meets the needs of our church on this project?

B. Contracts and Fees
1. What type owner-architect agreement would you propose? Can we have a copy for review?
2. Fees:
   a. How do you base your fee?
   b. When is it due?
   c. If it is based on a percentage, would you guarantee a maximum fee based on the scope of the project?
   d. What specifically is included in your basic fee? (Mechanical, electrical, plumbing, structural, acoustical, interior design, landscape design, color elevations, models, etc.)
   e. What is not included that we may need? What do you think it will cost?
3. Does your firm carry Errors and Omissions Insurance? Describe benefits of this coverage.

C. Timing
1. What is your estimate of the time required for each phase of the architectural and construction process?
2. Estimate the total time required for the project.

D. Cost Containment
1. What is the firm's record for designing within budget?
2. What factors will affect the balance between economy and quality?
3. Who is responsible for value engineering to bring the project within budget?

4. How would you propose client and architect work together to control costs of the project?

E. Construction Phase
1. What would your role be during the construction phase?
2. How often do you visit the construction site?
3. Do you have a preferred construction method?
4. What are some options for contractor selection?
5. How do you handle change orders, and how are they billed?

(The following copy should not be given to the architect.)

III. During the Interview

A. Listen for the architect's sensitivity to the church's needs and desires. How does he deal with unrealistic expectations by the committee? Does he reveal a healthy regard for work done by previous committees?
B. Does the architect listen and understand the committee?
C. Does he give evidence of being a good communicator?
D. Are suggestions and alternate approaches offered?
E. Does he seem familiar with local codes and buildings issues?

APPENDIX E

Special Promotion Helps

Events

Many events during a building program offer excellent opportunities to focus congregational and community attention on the proposed project. For example:

Site Dedication

The purchase of a site for a new work or for relocation can be magnified with a site dedication. This can signal the commitment of the church to begin a building project. (See suggestions in latter part of this appendix.)

Plans Presentation

Two or more presentations will likely be made: one at the time schematic plans are ready and another at the time the architect has developed the project design and a perspective. These presentations should be publicized so the larger community will be aware of the major facts of the project.

Awarding Construction Contract

Pictures and a news release can publicize the selection of the contractor and the awarding of the contract. Basic facts about the building can be included in this release. Celebrate the event as a significant step toward the realization of the church's dream.

Ground Breaking

This can be a significant time to emphasize the church's heritage and to further unite the congregation for the building project. Find ways to involve the congregation meaningfully in this celebration.

Laying the Cornerstone

Advance preparation will need to be made for the cornerstone and for the sealed receptacle containing mementos to be preserved. This event can be used to emphasize continuity with the past and commitment to the future.

Bolt and Beam Day

One church used the erection of a major beam as a time to focus attention on the new construction. The beam was described in detail and its importance to the structure emphasized.

Steeple Raising

Celebrating events such as this can be a way of keeping congregational interest in the building project at a significant level.

Anniversaries

Any significant anniversary in the life of the church can be utilized to mark and promote important aspects of the building program.

Lessons of fidelity and commitment can be drawn from the church's history and application can be made to the present challenge.

Homecoming

When this event occurs during the building program, a significant fund-raising emphasis will usually be successful. This can be a high hour of celebration and affirmation.

Departure Day

The last services in church facilities should be times of praise for blessings experienced there and times of dedication for the challenge of the future. Don't focus on the past. Call the congregation to new achievements and new victories.

Moving Day

Make the most of the move to new facilities. Remember the most important preparation for this time can be saturation visitation of all prospects. The church which moves into new facilities with record crowds will be well on its way to reaching new heights.

Open House

This is a time to reach out to the community and invite them to see the new facilities. Schedule this for a Sunday afternoon so other congregations can participate.

Dedication

Some churches have a dedication day. Others have a full week with special services on Sunday through Friday. Still others extend dedication over a full month with an emphasis on each Sunday. The main dedication service is usually planned for a Sunday morning worship service.

Note Burning

When the final payment on the mortgage has been made, many churches schedule a special service and symbolically burn the mortgage. A word of caution should be sounded. An emphasis on burning the mortgage and the fact that all indebtedness has been paid can lead to decreased giving. Guard against this by holding up a goal and a dream for the church to continue to pursue.

Special Program Suggestions

Site Dedication

Hymn "For the Beauty of the Earth"
Prayer
Scripture Psalm 24
Recognitions
Anthem
Dedication Message
Responsive Reading
Leader:

Yours, O Lord, is the greatness and the power and the glory and the majesty and the splendor, for everything in heaven and earth is Yours.

People:

Yours, O Lord, is the kingdom; You are exalted as head over all.

Leader:

Wealth and honor come from You; You are the ruler of all things. In Your hands are strength and power to exalt and give strength to all.

People:

Now, our God, we give You thanks, and praise Your glorious name.

Leader:

But who am I, and who are my people, that we should be able to give as generously as this? Everything comes from You, and we have given You only what comes from Your hand.

People:

We are aliens and strangers in Your sight, as were our forefathers. Our days on the earth are like a shadow, without hope (1 Chron. 29:11-15).

Leader:

That the faith of our forefathers may be remembered, and within us continued;

People:

We dedicate this ground.

Leader:

That by act, thought, and deed, we may continue to serve You and others in Your name;

People:

We dedicate this ground.

Leader:

To the glory of God, in the love of our Lord Jesus Christ, and through the grace of the Holy Spirit;

People:

We dedicate this ground.

Dedication Prayer

Hymn "Higher Ground"

Benediction

Ground-breaking Ceremony

Doxology
Invocation
Hymn "Lead On, O King Eternal"
Statement of Purpose
Pastor
Chair of Building-Steering Committee
Special Music
Responsive Scripture Reading

Leader:
Therefore everyone who hears these words of mine and puts them into practice is like a wise man who built his house on the rock.

People:
The rain came down, the streams rose, and the winds blew and beat against that house; yet it did not fall, because it had its foundation on the rock.

Leader:
But everyone who hears these words of mine and does not put them into practice is like a foolish man who built his house on sand.

People:
The rain came down, the streams rose, and the winds blew and beat against that house, and it fell with a great crash (Matt. 7:24-27).

Leader:
Sow for yourselves righteousness, reap the fruit of unfailing love, and . . .

People:
Break up your unplowed ground; for it is time to seek the Lord, until he comes and showers righteousness on you (Hos. 10:12).

Words of Challenge
Responsive Commitment

Leader:
That the faith of our forefathers may be remembered and within us continued and caused to shine;

People:
We break this ground.
Leader:
That by thought, word, and deed we may more faithfully serve our Lord;
People:
We break this ground.
Leader:
That we with joy may learn of His love and lead others to experience His saving power;
People:
We break this ground.
Leader:
To the glory of God, in the love of Jesus Christ, and by the grace of the Holy Spirit;
People:
We break this ground.
All:
Bless us this day, O Lord, and guide us in straight paths, that what we begin here today may be all to Your honor and glory; both now and forever. Amen
Leader:
Then shall the spade be put into the ground and the ground be broken, and we shall know that a good work is well begun.
Breaking Ground
A Charter Member
Chair of Deacons
Newest Member
Pastor
(Have each turn a spade of dirt and give a brief expression of commitment.)
Hymn "Onward Christian Soldiers"
Benediction

Laying the Cornerstone

Scripture Responses:
Leader:
Let the temple be rebuilt as a place to present sacrifices, and let its foundations be laid (Ezra 6:4).

People:

This is what the Sovereign Lord says; "See, I lay a stone in Zion, a tested stone, a precious cornerstone for a sure foundation" (Isa. 28:16)

Leader:

The Lord has done this, and it is marvelous in our eyes. This is the day the Lord has made; let us rejoice and be glad in it (Ps. 118:23-23).

People:

In the beginning, O Lord, you laid the foundations of the earth, and the heavens are the work of your hands. They will perish, but you remain; they will all wear out like a garment. . . . But you remain the same, and your years will never end (Heb. 1:10-12)

Leader:

God's solid foundation stands firm, sealed with this inscription: "The Lord knows those who are his" (2 Tim. 2:19)

People:

You are no longer foreigners and aliens, but fellow citizens with God's people and members of God's household, built on the foundation of the apostles and prophets, with Christ Jesus himself as the chief cornerstone. In him the whole building is joined together and rises to become a holy temple in the Lord. And in him you too are being built together to become a dwelling in which God lives by his Spirit (Eph. 2:19-22).

Hymn "Christ Is Made the Sure Foundation"
Invocation and Lord's Prayer
A Word on Behalf of the Community —A Civic Leader
A Word on Behalf of the Church —Pastor
A Word on Behalf of the Denomination
—A Denominational Leader
Depositing Articles in Receptacle —Selected Persons
Sealing Receptacle and Placing Inside Stone
—Chair of Building-Steering Committee
Presentation of Trowel to Person to Set Stone
Laying the Cornerstone
Prayer of Dedication
The Doxology
Benediction

Service of Dedication

Call to Worship
Invocation
Hymn "All Hail the Power of Jesus Name"
Responsive Reading
Hymn "Built on the Rock"
Vows of Dedication

Pastor:

Since God in His wisdom has led us in the building of this house and in His mercy has brought us to its completion, let us now proceed to dedicate it to Him. To the glory of God the Father, to the honor of His Son, and to the praise of the Holy Spirit;

People:

We dedicate this building.

Pastor:

Believing in God the Father, in whom we live and move and have our being, and from whom comes every good and perfect gift,

People:

We dedicate this building to the worship of God in praise and prayer, to the preaching of the everlasting gospel, and to the observance of the ordinances.

Pastor:

For the comfort of all who mourn,
For strength to those who are tempted,
For a lift to those who are distressed,
For light to those who seek the way;

People:

We dedicate this building.

Pastor:

For the hallowing of family life,
For the teaching and guidance of youth,
For the edification and growth of Christians,

People:

We dedicate this building.

Pastor:
For the conversion of sinners,
For the promotion of righteousness,
For the extension of the kingdom of God;
People:
We dedicate this building.
Pastor:
In loving memory of those who have gone from us, whose hearts and hands have served in this church; with gratitude for all whose faith and consecrated gifts make this house possible; in gratitude for the labors of all those who love and serve this church, and with prayer for all who shall worship in this house in years to come;
People:
We dedicate this building.
All:
We, the people of this church and congregation, do now dedicate ourselves anew to the worship of God in this place and to the great work to which He has called us.

Dedication Prayer
Anthem
Message
Hymn "Lead On, O King Eternal"
Benediction